ZEN SPIRIT, CHRISTIAN SPIRIT

ZEN SPIRIT, CHRISTIAN SPIRIT

The Place of Zen in Christian Life

ROBERT E. KENNEDY

CONTINUUM • NEW YORK

1995

The Continuum Publishing Company
370 Lexington Avenue
New York, NY 10017

Printed in the United States of America

Library of Congress Cataloging-in-Publication Data

Kennedy, Robert E., 1933–
    Zen spirit, Christian spirit : the place of Zen in Christian life
    / Robert E. Kennedy.
        p.   cm.
    ISBN 0-8264-0806-0
    1. Spiritual life—Zen Buddhism. 2. Spiritual life—Catholic
Church. 3. Zen Buddhism—Relations—Catholic Church. 4.
Catholic Church—Relations—Zen Buddhism. 5. Kennedy,
Robert E., 1933–   .
    I. Title.
BQ9269.4.C35K46   1995   95-6153
261.2'43927—dc20   CIP

All biblical references come from *The Jerusalem Bible,* copyright
1966, 1967, and 1968 by Darton, Longman & Todd Ltd. and
Doubleday & Company, Inc.

To all my teachers

Buddhist and Christian

Living and dead

It burns in the void

Nothing upholds it.

Still it travels.

—Kathleen Raine

ACKNOWLEDGMENTS

I am grateful to Teresita Fay, R.S.H.M., Doctor of English Literature and Principal at Arthur Andersen and Co., who not only took time from her busy life to edit these pages, but who offered counsel throughout that was always wise and wonderful.

My sisters Rene and Marjorie and my brother Bill and their families encouraged me in this enterprise, listened to me patiently, and offered loving hospitality. Bill, the author of several novels and screen plays, read the manuscript, believed in it, and gave me new life.

Many friends supported me with advice and encouragement: Bernard Glassman Tetsugen Sensei, Sr. Janet Richardson, Jinne Sensei, Ellen and Charles Birx, Niklaus Brantschen, Judith Bruder, Arnold Rachman, Rosemary O'Connell, and *in memoriam*, Rev. James E. Hennessy, S.J., 1913–1992, a wise and joyful friend.

Mrs. Peggy Greenwood of Saint Peter's College typed and retyped my handwritten pages and always seemed glad to see me.

CONTENTS

PART IV

GOLD: ACHIEVEMENT AND UNION

FOREWORD

Zen training has traditionally included two paths which are usually combined but not to be confused: the path of teacher and the path of the priest. The path of the Zen teacher is to fully realize, and then to transmit, the unconditional experience that is the essential core of Zen and, I believe, the core of all mystical traditions. One way to describe this unconditional experience is the seeing into our deepest nature as human beings and the realizing of the oneness of all life.

The path of the Zen priest is the clerical or liturgical path that celebrates the essential experience of the oneness of all life. The form of this liturgical celebration has evolved over many centuries in the Buddhist culture of China and Japan into traditional expressions of chant, dress, and lifestyle.

Robert Kennedy, already a Catholic priest, has not pursued the path to the Zen Buddhist priesthood, but rather has pursued the path of the lay Zen teacher: he has trained for twenty years with Zen teachers, he has been approved by them, and he has been installed as a Zen teacher himself.

For many years I have been convinced that the Zen experience can be celebrated not only in the Buddhist liturgies of China and Japan, but that the experience can also be realized by people of other faiths and celebrated in their own liturgical forms.

I am pleased to confirm that Robert Kennedy has accomplished these goals. He has plumbed the depths of the Zen teaching tradition without deviating from the Jesuit path to which he committed himself as a young man. He has celebrated the Catholic liturgy for us in the Zen Center in a manner that leads the participants to deepen their contemplative life. And he has written this book to help his readers undergo the process of spiritual alchemy that he so lucidly describes in these pages.

Having seen to the completion of his Zen training, I have fully entrusted him with the teaching of the White Plumb lineage transmitted to me by my own teacher, the Venerable Taizan Maezumi Roshi.

On behalf of this lineage, I feel greatly honored to have been able to help Robert Kennedy along the Zen path, and I look forward with excitement to see how his unique expression of the Dharma will manifest itself within the Catholic tradition.

I have given Robert Kennedy the name Jinsen, meaning the fountain of God or that place where God springs up in the world to be a source of light and peace to all. May this name be fulfilled in him in the years to come.

Bernard Tetsugen Glassman
Abbot of the Zen Center of New York

PREFACE

The journey of the author will be familiar to all who remember the pre-Vatican II Catholic Church. I was born in an Irish Catholic ghetto in Brooklyn, New York, to a devout family, and was educated by nuns and priests. And so it will come as no surprise to the reader that on graduating from a Jesuit high school, I immediately joined the Jesuits and vowed to stay there.

Nor will the reader familiar at all with the style of pre-Vatican II religious life be surprised that I volunteered to go to Japan to bring the Roman Catholic Church to the Japanese people.

And after several years of language study, English teaching, baseball coaching and pre-Vatican II theology, I was ordained a priest in Tokyo by Cardinal Doi in March 1965.

I was ordained in the teeth of the wind of Vatican II that blew away the form of the Catholic Church as I knew it. A sudden sea change should not frighten a sailor, but I was not one of those forward-looking Jesuits who knew what was wrong with the Church; nor did I delight in the upheaval that followed the Council. My temperament and training and my relative isolation in Japan on the fringe of the Church led me to cling to the only form of Catholic life I knew. I tried to be faithful to what I was taught, but finally the dike had more holes than I had fingers and the flood of changes in my life swept away my old religious certitudes. Most painfully, I lost my way in prayer. The precious words and images and the stately liturgy that sustained me for so long suddenly froze on my lips and in my heart. What a grace that was, though I didn't know it then.

And so, washed up on the beach with little saved from my religious shipwreck, I looked about for a fresh start. I completed doctoral studies in theology at Ottawa University. I entered a psychoanalytic training institute in New York City and asked only that my training analyst be Jewish. I also returned to Japan during a sabbatical year in 1976. This time I was not a missionary but a pilgrim, and I sought out those fellow Jesuits who were working and dialoguing with Zen Buddhist masters. I wanted to meet with and pray with those Zen masters who were revered for their depth of insight and discernment. How ironic it was that in my attempt to put a firm foundation under my religious life, I turned to a wisdom tradition that knew that there was no firm foundation to life and that there was nothing "religious" about life either. What a grace that was, though I didn't know it then.

During this pilgrim year in Japan, I was helped by two pairs of friendly hands. Fr. William Johnston, S.J., took time from his busy life to talk with me and explain that Zen was less a religion than a way of looking at life. Bill joined me on a trip to Kyoto where we walked under a blazing sun from temple to temple, sitting with any master who would have us. No footnote in the text that follows can express my gratitude for his rich companionship.

The second pair of friendly hands were those of Yamada Roshi of Kamakura. The term *roshi* is reserved for those few Zen teachers whose enlightened spirit is especially recognized by the community. Yamada Roshi radiated an enlightened and fruitful life, and to my delight he accepted me as his student, a Christian and a complete beginner who knew nothing at all.

These were wonderful days sitting with Yamada Roshi and the students. Each morning I took the train from Tokyo to Kamakura and sat all day until the roshi returned from work. Then the roshi would instruct us individually and have tea with us all as a group.

Fifteen years later when Glassman Sensei, my American Zen teacher in New York, told me I was to become a teacher myself, my first thought was to call Yamada Roshi, but I had learned he had just died in Kamakura. The next summer, 1990, I visited Mrs. Yamada in Kamakura and tried to tell her all her

husband meant to me, but tears came instead of words. To paraphrase an old Japanese poet:

> Yamada Roshi,
> the branches stir the breeze
> to bid you farewell.

Since my installation as a Zen teacher in New York in December 1991, I have been asked by Zen practitioners if I had
lost my Catholic faith and didn't know it, or if I had lost it and
didn't have the courage to admit it. As far as anyone can
answer a question like that, I never have thought of myself as
anything but Catholic and I certainly never have thought of
myself as a Buddhist. What I lost was a Catholic culture that
has now all but disappeared from the American scene. I learned
painfully that faith is never to be identified with the cultural
forms of any given age, and especially so when that cultural
form is taken for granted and deeply loved. While this simple
truth may be obvious to the reader, in my experience it was a
truth burned into my soul.

What I looked for in Zen was not a new faith, but a new way
of being Catholic that grew out of my own lived experience and
would not be blown away again by authority or by changing theological fashion.

Specifically, I looked for two things. First, to the extent that
Buddhism is a great world religion, I was looking for a life of
interreligious dialogue. I wanted to be in close communion with
men and women who searched for the truth of their lives with
such energy that I believe Jesus would say of them, "I have not
found such faith in Israel." The Church admits more freely
today than ever before that grace and truth and salvation are
found in Buddhism and therefore Catholics should approach
Buddhism not uncritically but with hope and anticipation. In
the Yamauchi lectures of the spring of 1994, Stephen Duffy of
Loyola University writes that Jesus as a "marginal Jew" could
not possibly be the sole medium of grace. There was grace and
truth before Jesus, and there is grace and truth in the world
that cannot know Jesus now. We recognize that what we have in
Jesus may be represented for others by another symbol. Jesus is
the perfect expression of the Father, but not the only expression
of the Father. To quote Duffy directly:

> The Christian claim that Jesus is decisive is not a claim that
> God is to be found only in Jesus and nowhere else, but that
> the only God that might possibly be discovered elsewhere is
> the God made known in the life and death of Jesus.[1]

Therefore interreligious dialogue with Buddhism means for me
an opportunity to share in the Church's ongoing reconstruction
of itself as Catholic.

Secondly, and more to the point, Zen Buddhism need not be
looked at as a religion at all, but as a way of seeing life that can
enhance any religious faith. Yamada Roshi told me several
times he did not want to make me a Buddhist but rather he
wanted to empty me in imitation of "Christ your Lord" who
emptied himself, poured himself out, and clung to nothing.
Whenever Yamada Roshi instructed me in this way, I thought
that this Buddhist might make a Christian of me yet!

And so I do not relate to Zen as an alien religion, but as an
opportunity to share with like-minded men and women of many
religions a way of being human; I know that nothing truly
human can be alien to the Church or to me. Neither Yamada
Roshi nor any other Zen teacher I worked with ever asked me
about my faith. Rather they asked me how I sat, how I
breathed, and how I saw the world. We met on the common
ground of human experience that gradually became clearer and
fresher.

This book is an extension of many conversations I have had
with members of my Catholic family of Jesuit, religious, and lay
men and women interested in Zen meditation. But I write not
only for Catholics, but for anyone from a theistic tradition who
wishes to make sense of a non-theistic Zen form of seeing and
living life. Many sincere believers in God come up against the
limits that their culture has imposed on their faith. They find
they want to believe and hope and pray, but they can no longer
accept faith that they perceive is based on untested authority,
or on miracles, apparitions, private revelations, or a literal
reading of Scripture that borders on the fantastic. Many gifted
adult Catholics sadly walk away from the Church because they
have not found a vision of Catholicism that they can integrate
into their mature experience of life. They are not interested in a
new faith, or in watering down an old faith, or in arguing with

authority figures about moral issues or old heresies. In Zen they can find their own path, one that leads them to self-knowledge, deeper prayer, and lively service of others.

Is there danger that a Catholic would be "led astray" by Zen practice? Well, of course there is! There is danger even that the celebration of the liturgy could degenerate into "magic" unless there is sound guidance given to beginners. No religious practice is free from distortion, and that is why the Church needs teachers competent in both Catholic and Zen practice who can respond to the needs of the faithful who are drawn to this form of prayer and life.

Zen Buddhism is here to stay in the United States; it will attract an increasing number of thoughtful Christians and it does not seem pastorally wise to ignore it or be ignorant of it. Zen differs profoundly from Christianity. It was spawned in a different century; it asked different questions of life and gave different answers. But not every Zen teaching is opposed to Christian faith, and some Zen insights can be most helpful to Christians and might even in the future be taught by the Church as her own. Even where Zen and Christianity differ, surely that difference should not keep us from cooperating on all the work we do in common for the benefit of humanity. If our goal is to argue with Zen, we can do so forever. But if our goal is to learn as well as to teach, then their door is open for us to come and sit with them. What is the alternative? Do we wish to say that the Church has nothing to learn from Asia?

Let us hear from Asia on Buddhist Christian dialogue. In mid-September 1994, His Holiness the Dalai Lama spoke before an audience of 250 Christians at Middlesex University, London. The occasion was the John Main Seminar, sponsored by the World Community for Christian Meditation, and the Dalai Lama was asked to comment on passages from the Christian Scriptures. Writing in London for *The Tablet*, Robert Kiely noted that it was impossible not to be moved, almost stunned by the power of familiar words re-cadenced by a Tibetan voice and a Buddhist sensibility.[2] Some of the Christians present said later that it was as if they were hearing the words for the first time, as though their tenderness and mystery and beauty had been taken for granted, and were brought to life again, like a gift from an unexpected courier. Kiely stresses that what impressed and surprised the listeners was that it was an outsider with no authority over Christians except what was given by the Spirit and that he was able to show them the riches of their own banquet.

At the same time the Dalai Lama again and again counseled people that human sensibilities and cultures are too varied to justify a single way to the truth. He resisted all suggestions that Buddhism and Christianity are different languages for the same essential beliefs and said that the two faiths are so different that those who call themselves "Buddhist-Christians" are trying "to put a yak's head on a sheep's body."[3] Behind the enlightening teaching and wise caution of the Dalai Lama, I heard again the words of Yamada Roshi to me: "I am not trying to make you a Buddhist, but to empty you in imitation of your Lord Jesus Christ."

ABOUT THE BOOK

I would like to caution the reader that this book is neither an instruction on Zen Buddhism nor is it an explanation of the koans. Zen students have their own teachers and their own methods of practice. Nor is this book an introduction to Christian life or prayer. Most of the Christians who come to the Zen Center of New York are quite knowledgeable in the teachings of their faith. Rather in this book, as in my talks at the Zen center, I emphasize some aspects of Zen Buddhism that attempt to answer the many questions Christians themselves have about Zen and Christianity. Often in my talks I explain to Christians that Zen is, in part, a non-theistic form of human development which is nurtured within Buddhism, but which is available to all who are willing and able to submit to its discipline.

I personally have experienced that the practice of Zen, under the guidance of a teacher, can be integrated into Christian life; it can deepen Christian prayer and root our faith not just in our head but in our whole person. Christians need not be surprised that something like Zen can be integrated into Christian life and deepen it. The Declaration on Non-Christian Religions explains that the Catholic religion rejects nothing of all that which is true and holy in these religions. Not only does the Church not reject what is true and holy in non-Christian religions, but it encourages us to seek out positively and accept whatever they possess that is true and holy. The Church that is always to be reformed needs the prophetic corrective of prophets in the Church and prophets outside the Church, among whom the Buddha should be included par excellence.[1]

The spiritual life has been divided traditionally into four stages of human growth: knowledge, love, purification, and union. These four stages have been compared to the four stages of alchemy: lead, quicksilver, sulphur, and gold. Accordingly, I have divided the structure of this book as follows:

Part I: Lead—The Darkness of Knowledge and Theory;
Part II: Quicksilver—The Poetry of Inspiration and Desire;
Part III: Sulphur—The Fire of Practice and Transformation;
Part IV: Gold—Achievement and Union.

In "Part I: Lead—The Darkness of Knowledge and Theory," I have attempted to bring together the Zen teaching of Thomas Merton and William Johnston with *The Cloud of Unknowing* and my own reflections on more than twenty years of Zen experience. Theology is not to everyone's taste, but in this part I have tried to answer all the questions that Christians have asked me during the years I taught at the Zen Center of New York.

In "Part II: Quicksilver—The Poetry of Inspiration and Desire," and throughout the text, I have used poetry and literature to illustrate Zen teaching. Zen teachers do not lecture their students; instead they try to evoke insight by the skillful use of beauty. Indeed beauty and wisdom perish in the same ignorance.

In "Part III: Sulphur—The Fire of Practice and Transformation," I have used Zen koans to suggest where Zen can affirm and deepen Christian life. Insight is born in the fire of practice.

And in "Part IV: Gold—Achievement and Union," I recall a Sufi myth that suggests that God's final revelation is we ourselves.

PART I

LEAD

THE DARKNESS
OF KNOWLEDGE AND THEORY

For whom is the elaborate toilette now discarded?
The cuckoo's call urges the traveler to turn home.
Its note continues when all flowers have fallen,
Echoing deep among the intermingling peaks.

ABOUT BUDDHISM

Shortly after World War II, *The Harp of Burma* was published in Japan. This novel relates the story of a young Japanese harpist and soldier who survives the destruction of the Japanese army in Burma and who remains in that country to become a Buddhist monk. The first third of the book deals with this sensitive young man's arrival in Burma and describes the willing part he plays in the Japanese occupation. The author describes the harpist as nationalistic, efficient, and obedient and informs the reader that this young soldier's life is shaped by Shinto: he is a child of the clan who has to fight in defense of the clan. The war song of the Shinto clan claims that the soldier must not only face the flying arrows but also rejoice if he should die in his dread Sovereign's cause. As one can conclude, Shinto means not only adherence to aesthetics but also, and very importantly, commitment to the use of the sword whenever called upon to do so.

The second third of the book begins with the catastrophic arrival of the British, who rout the Japanese army in Burma and take the young harpist-hero prisoner. The British give him a shovel and force him to bury his own dead comrades. This horrible experience transforms him completely. No longer does he see himself simply as a follower in his sovereign's cause; he now recognizes a depth to life beyond obedient soldiering. He resolves not to return to Japan until he understands the meaning of life and death. He slips away, finds a Buddhist community, and becomes a monk. This phase of his life is shaped by Buddhism, by the experience of suffering. He is determined to see into the meaning of life, to understand suffering and to alleviate it.

The last part of the novel focuses on the efforts of his friends to get the young harpist to abandon his religious search, to accept his civic duty, and to return to rebuild Japan. His friends appeal to his relational responsibility to his government, parents, and friends: that is, to the Confucian side of his Japanese personality. However, in spite of their effort, the harpist's concentration on the Buddhist quest for wisdom and insight is all-consuming. He remains a seeker in Burma while his friends march home.

The theme of *The Harp of Burma* recalls the life of the historical Buddha. Twenty-five centuries before the novel was written, a young prince and chieftain in what is now Nepal lived a successful and privileged life. His life changed suddenly when what had always been unseen before his eyes came into focus. Suffering, in the form of sickness, old age, and death, became real to him and he could not go on living as he had until he could understand and alleviate it.

Like many who start out on this path, but whose good intentions become distracted, the Buddha too was sorely tempted, as the myth recalls, by the attractive sons and voluptuous daughters of Lord Death. His final temptation, to fulfill his duty to his caste, to society, and to civic responsibility, was the sharpest. He was tempted to give up his search for wisdom and to build something. However, not unlike the hero of *The Harp of Burma*, Buddha possessed a sensitivity which forced him to stay the course. The mythic Lord Death with his army of frightening and tempting forms disappeared; symbolically, a full moon rose and Buddha received complete insight into the structure of life.

One might wonder about the insight of the Buddha and the young Japanese harpist, questioning the importance of this insight and asking what insight into the structure of life means. Yamada Roshi, with whom I practiced Zen in Kamakura twenty years ago, never tired of teaching that without this insight there is no Buddhism. He emphasized that all the masters and patriarchs throughout the history of Buddhism, including Dogen Zenji and Hakuin Zenji, taught the same thing. Yamada Roshi became alarmed at the thought of any master teaching Buddhism without focusing on this insight which so enabled/empowered the Buddha and the young Japanese harpist.

Buddhists call this insight *kensho*, which means seeing into the nature of the world. And what is the nature of the world? Teachers vary in the emphasis they give to their experience of *kensho*, but they all agree on this: first, all the objects of our faculties—all that we see and hear and feel and touch and think and imagine—all these objects are in fact not objects at all. Instead they are one with the self. These teachers insist that there is no objective world independent of the self. All forms are empty. Second, the subject too, the perceiving self, is equally empty. There is no unchanging, permanent center or soul. No one perceives the objective emptiness. Subjectively, all forms are empty. The subject and the object are one in emptiness. Third, this empty oneness of subject and object is nothing more than the constantly changing phenomenal world of forms, colors, and sensations which constantly rise and fall according to the law of causation. There is no emptiness existing by itself. The emptiness exists only as form.

It is a simple matter to write down these brief statements, to understand them, and even to teach them. But to experience their reality is to experience the universe, as we know it, in collapse. This is what happened to the Buddha and to the young Japanese harpist. Commenting on his own experience of *kensho*, Yamada Roshi reminds us of the Buddha and the Japanese harpist. Seeing into the nature of the world, Yamada Roshi exclaimed in great wonder and delight that that which he was told by all the patriarchs down through Yasuntani Roshi was true. His life was totally transformed. He experienced the meaning of human existence, and this insight enabled him to alleviate the suffering, anxiety, and fear of those who came to him for counsel.

ABOUT ZEN

Buddhism is the first world religion known to history. It bridges all the differences which exist in the unique and creative cultures of India, Indochina, Indonesia, China, Tibet, Korea, and Japan. It is the most representative religion of Asia.

The growth of Buddhism, the various forms it took in different cultures, the development of the Mahayana School, the rise of what is now known as Zen Buddhism in China and its transplantation to Japan are far beyond the intent of this book. My purpose is to introduce Zen to the Christian reader. Let me begin by briefly summarizing some of the thoughts of the Zen master Hakuin who lived in the Tokugawa period in Japan from 1686 to 1769. His greatness continues to influence all present-day masters of his school who trace themselves back to him.

In his time Hakuin, a humanist, rejected the pessimism about humanity that characterized some Buddhist schools during his era. There were Buddhists who believed that men and women were not capable of saving themselves by means of traditional discipline and meditation. They believed that human, physical, moral, and spiritual capacities were so corrupted that men and women needed to rely on some other power, the Buddha, to save them.

Hakuin believed that such pessimistic theories made it too easy for us not to take the responsibility for our own lives, a responsibility he believed necessary for enlightenment. Hakuin believed that these pessimistic theories too easily led people to grovel in self-pity and to make excuses for their failures.

He wrote:

Such (pessimistic) people are known as destroyers and wasters
of their own selves. . . . They are like fish in water who lament
the fact that because of their natures they are unable to see
the water or like birds flying through the air who regret the
fact that to see the air is an unattainable desire. . . .[1]

Now let us briefly look at Hakuin's understanding of faith.
Hakuin taught that there was no Buddha independent of one's
mind who would come to save the person. Hakuin believed that
salvation could only be achieved by people seeing into their own
nature. For Hakuin this experience always led to the discovery
that the human mind and the Buddha's mind were the same
mind. Hakuin encouraged men and women to discover the
Buddha nature within themselves and all things, for no one else
could make this discovery for them. Likewise, according to
Hakuin, great faith in some external power was no substitute
for total self-effort.

Hakuin ridiculed the psychological and ontological dualism
implied in people calling on the Buddha to take them to a Pure
Land and to turn them into Buddhas. He wrote:

What is this "going"? What is this "becoming"? If this isn't ego,
(and dualism) then what is it?[2]

Hakuin's teaching on the nature of salvation flowed from
his understanding of non-duality. For him, there was no one
outside the self that humanity could pray to; there was no other
place one could go to for salvation. This great Zen master
believed that salvation meant one thing—seeing into our own
nature, which is always with us and standing right before our
very eyes. If we do not attain this insight, then mumbling endless prayers will not bring us to the Pure Land.

Hakuin defined salvation as:

. . . the state of mind in which you are not a man, not a woman;
you do not see birth, you do not see death; and in which there
is only vast emptiness, where the distinction between night
and day is not seen and the body and mind are lost.[3]

Hakuin had only pity for those who trusted that there was
a Buddha in some Pure Land to whom humanity, by calling on

his name, could somehow be born again with the Buddha after death.

Finally, immortality for Hakuin was not an endless life after death. For him life and death were not two separate things. According to Hakuin we are not moving from life to death to perpetual life; instead, we are living and at the same time dying. At every moment we are all life and all death. Our life is not a movement toward death but a continual process of living and dying. Hakuin believed in a paradoxical and dynamic oneness of life and death.

This living-dying in Zen is neither process nor continuity. If we realize that we are living and dying at every moment, then we will understand that this existence itself is death. It is not death as opposed to life, but death in an absolute sense. It is called the Great Death, and at the very moment one dies the Great Death, Great Life manifests itself and one can live one's living-dying existence without becoming shackled by it.

Zen teaches that our living-dying existence is without beginning, end, or history. This living-dying existence has no single center. Accordingly, every point in history is a center. If one is alert and lives Great Life through Great Death at every moment, one is always in the center.

Zen, therefore, does not look for immortality of the soul or for eternal life in the Pure Land, but for a salvation in which living-dying itself is completely abolished. Zen teaches that today does not bring us closer to eternity; because today, at this moment, eternity is completely manifesting itself. We are experiencing eternity today.

And what happens after physical death? Hakuin and his followers would say that we lose all individuality at the moment of death and so become untraceable. We discard everything which is not pure absolute. Hence, since the terms of individuality no longer apply to us, it would be impossible to say anything about us. To speak of one after physical death is to speak of the Absolute. And to speak of the Absolute is comparable to trying to "trap a scent with one's hands."[4]

The Zen novice is constantly told that the self does not exist and that its illusion must be annihilated. And, indeed, at the moment of enlightenment one actually experiences the truth of this belief. Though the Christian may insist that this is a misinterpretation of experience, the Zen enlightened person has no doubt that the experience itself is one of absolute unity.

In Zen, "one's own nature" is often called the Buddha-nature. The Buddha-nature is what is intrinsic to all sentient beings: that is, all existence. Human beings, animals, and plants are the Buddha-nature equally though they may not necessarily be aware of it. This does not mean that all sentient beings merely *have* the Buddha-nature hidden within them; it does mean that there *is* only the Buddha-nature and nothing else.

The fundamental doctrine of Buddhism teaches that the substance of all existence is emptiness. This emptiness is the living, dynamic, formless source of all existence; it exists beyond individuality or personality; it is unimaginable, inconceivable, and capable of endless transformation. For the Buddhist, all the forms of this world are illusory in that they have no abiding substance; the root substance of all reality is emptiness.

This basic doctrine of Buddhism is explained at times by the law of dependent origination and at other times by the law of the middle way. The law of dependent origination maintains that every apparently fixed form is actually impermanent and unsubstantial. The law of the middle way claims that one who sees the emptiness of these forms does not believe in their existence. In other words, the cosmos is conditional, relational, and dependent. Hence, because this exists, that exists. But nothing exists in or by itself. There is no self.

However, since the Buddha-nature is unimaginable and inconceivable, the Zen Buddhists maintain that these laws are merely a hazy portrait of the Buddha-nature. The laws do not teach us how to realize our true nature, nor do they liberate our mind from the snare of language and concepts which fit over experience and blind us to it. They do not loosen our hold on dogmas, our tendency to judge good from bad, or our ideas of the self and other. For true liberation, which goes beyond the law, Zen practice is essential.

ZEN PRACTICE

Zen practice helps us to realize our true nature and to liberate our mind from concepts and images. It does this through
the habitual practice of *zazen*, especially during the *sesshin*, a
week-long retreat. One of the essential elements of the *sesshin* is
the retreatant's intense concentration on *zazen:* the act of
straight-backed sitting and rhythmic breathing which help unify
and control the mind through sustained concentration. Two other
main elements of the *sesshin* which also foster self-realization
are: *teisho*, the roshi's formal talk to the retreatants, who, while
he or she speaks, continue to sit upright and listen with uninter-
rupted concentration; and *dokusan*, the retreatant's face-to-face
encounter with the roshi in the privacy of the roshi's room.

Both my study of these three elements and my personal
experience of them during the many *sesshin* I have made confirm my belief in their effectiveness. The daily twelve hours of
zazen, though agonizingly long, dreaded, yet paradoxically
desired, help the retreatant to empty her mind of all thoughts,
images, feelings, anxieties, and desires, even of the desire for
enlightenment itself. In Zen, the conscious mind must be
brought to a standstill and remain in total darkness. Although
one might think that such a mind, totally emptied, would lapse
into unconsciousness or sleep, this does not happen. Rather a
new type of concentration sets in and the mind works vigorously at another level. Its attention is not dispersed but is con-
centrated on emptiness.

The first aim of this sitting is to unify the mind and make it
one-pointed so that it is not pulled about by the compulsive and
repetitious chatter we are all familiar with. In order to unify

the mind, the beginner is instructed to count each breath and become one with it. As concentration deepens, one discovers that it is impossible to distinguish oneself from the breathing. If, however, the counting is distracting, one may "just sit." Whether one counts each breath or not, the mind must be unhurried, firm, and composed; it must be stretched like a taut bowstring. Either method will do as long as the mind remains alert and without images. Because such concentration cannot usually be maintained for more than thirty minutes at a time, a bell is sounded for all to rise and process around the hall. This walking is to relax the muscles without breaking the concentration, which is to continue throughout the day.

There are two aids to concentration. The first is the stick, which is used vigorously across the shoulders during *zazen* to tap every vestige of dormant energy in the retreatant. It rouses us when we are sleepy, puts new life into us when we are weary; it spurs us on when we are close to success. The second is the retreatant's own fidelity to the rules and procedures of the meditation hall. These include the detailed ritual for meals in which every particle of food is carefully scraped and eaten, including the film left in the bowl; the chanting of the *Sutras*; the exact etiquette of bowing and walking; the correct position of the eyes, hands, and fingers; and the rules for the toilet and for sleeping. The importance of such observances can be detected in the words of Maezumi Roshi, who claims that we express our inner state at every turn and insists that if our actions are sloppy, our understanding and our whole life will show it.

When a retreatant has some success with breathing and sitting, he is usually given a problem called a koan. The koan is an illogical puzzle that traps the understanding mind in such a way that, unable to find an outlet, it is overcome with almost intolerable anguish. According to one theory, the mind experiences an inner explosion of insight: namely, enlightenment. But the retreatant must absorb the koan without concepts or reasoning. Only when his mind is emptied of all ideas can the retreatant respond to the koan with his whole being, and not just with his head. Hence he must live in darkness, for enlightenment will come out of this darkness, and not from the light of reason.

There are hundreds of koans that have been developed throughout the centuries, but the koan *mu* is by far the one most used by the masters in training their monks. It is very brief and goes as follows: A monk in all seriousness asked Joshu, his master: "Has a dog the Buddha-nature or not? Joshu retorted '*mu*'." The master would not say whether the dog did or did not have Buddha-nature because everything *is* Buddha-nature. His answer, therefore, is simply *mu*, a meaningless sound that had nothing to do with have or have not. *Mu* is itself the Buddha-nature and it thrusts this truth before us.

To penetrate the meaning of *mu* one must achieve absolute unity with it and hold fast to it night and day. In his uncritical but questioning absorption with *mu*, the retreatant no longer perceives a duality between himself and the *mu* koan. On the contrary, he becomes *mu* so that it is *mu* that eats, *mu* that walks, *mu* that sleeps and awakens. In the words of Yamada Roshi, it is finally no longer the retreatant who enters his door, but *mu*.

In his teaching, Yamada Roshi encouraged us to ignore the distractions that came to us and to simply return to *mu*. This constant returning to *mu*, he claimed, is excellent *zazen*. And so from 4:00 A.M. to 9:00 P.M. during a *sesshin* I attended with Yamada Roshi, the other retreatants and I struggled from one long, painful period of *zazen* to another, ignoring the familiar stream of thoughts, the emotions of elation and discouragement, and continually returning to *mu*. During that *sesshin* the director of one hall scolded us for our lazy and half-hearted attempts at striving for enlightenment. He did this during *zazen* in order to prod us on to enlightenment. "What have you come for?" he would cry and then continue, "unless you do better, you will lose the most precious experience in the world. Do not split your attention; only when you are mindless and selfless will *mu* spring forth."

The *teisho*, the second element of the *sesshin*, is different from an academic lecture which explains the meaning of a text from Scripture. It is the dramatization of the point of the particular koan the roshi comments upon. He or she often impersonates the roles of its dialogue to nudge the listeners toward an intuition of its truth.

The third element of the *sesshin*, the *dokusan*, is of great benefit to the retreatant. What is said in *dokusan* is, of course, always unique according to the ability and progress of the student, and according to the methods and personality of the roshi. I have found that no matter what is the personality of the roshi, each seems to radiate two qualities during *dokusan*: an absolute confidence in method and an encouraging spirit.

During my *sesshin* under the guidance of Yamada Roshi, he assured us that if we followed his directions, we would see the meaning of life to its very root. This is very much like the teaching of Yasuntani Roshi, the one who brought Yamada Roshi himself to enlightenment, who explained that with enlightenment a Zen student would know down to her bowels the meaning of human existence. In both cases the roshi's certainty rested on the fact that he had an experience which the student still lacked. Thus the role of the roshi is to lead the student step by step along the path to enlightenment, answering the latter's questions and responding to her needs with a care and concern which is tempered with a commanding decisiveness.

It is because of his or her own clarity and confidence that the roshi can be so encouraging to the retreatant. While it is true that a roshi is not necessary for the beginning student (a good teacher can tell one how to sit and correct basic mistakes), nevertheless, the roshi's presence is inspirational to this same beginner who struggles with pain, frustration, and boredom. During my first *sesshin,* I asked Yamada Roshi if it were permissible to come to *dokusan* even when I had nothing to say, "Yes, of course," the roshi answered. "Come for inspiration."

ZEN AND CHRISTIANITY

Writing of the difficulty of comparing Zen to Christianity, Thomas Merton, in his introduction to John Wu's *The Golden Age of Zen*, tells us that to compare them is like comparing tennis to mathematics.[5] Accordingly, not all Christians will be interested in practicing Zen because of its disagreement with Christianity on theological and philosophical issues. Even though that may indeed be the case, I would like to suggest that Zen can remind us of essential truths in our own Christian religion which, because of our contemporary social preoccupations, we tend to forget. For example, many Christians are not interested in contemplative prayer, which is actually the point where Zen and Christianity can converge. But a vast majority of Christians believe that their salvation lies not in the depth of their prayer, but solely in the practice of charity. Even those who hold authority in the Church make no claim to any contemplative enlightenment.

Still, the Church has always greatly valued the contemplative aspiration; I contend that there are aspects of our contemplative prayer life which could be enriched by a study of Zen. Not only Zen, but our own traditional, verbal, image-filled, Christian prayers and meditations should lead us to deeper, more contemplative prayer. For, although meditation on the words of Scripture and revelation are helpful to the Christian, especially to the beginner, we can achieve true meditation only when we really grasp the truths of Scripture and revelation. We become aware that Christ's purpose was to reveal these truths. Once we see these truths with the eyes of faith, our will goes out in love to the mystery they express. This is the beginning of contemplative prayer: an empty and imageless prayer which is the naked intent of the will reaching out to God, not as I imagine him to be, or as he is in any of his works, but as he is in himself.

So life-giving is this imageless contemplation that, according to Thomas Merton in *Contemplative Prayer*, when it is absent, religion itself tends to lose its consistency and truth. Merton writes that it is the contemplative, silent, "empty," and apparently useless element in the life of prayer which makes it truly a life. Without contemplation liturgy tends to be a mere pious show: paraliturgical prayer becomes plain babbling and mental prayer, nothing but a sterile exercise of the mind.

Although this teaching about contemplative prayer is commonly accepted in the Church, it is not so commonly put into practice; it is precisely here that Zen can be of great help to those Christians who desire to deepen their contemplative life. For Zen is a way of contemplation that psychologically has much in common with true Christian prayer. And since as a way of contemplation, as Yamada Roshi and others say, it can be used without reference to its theological background, it can teach Christians a way to pray that is imageless, silent, and conducive to unifying the Christian personality in a radical detachment from all things.

This attempt to unify the personality in radical detachment from all things seems at first to be a cold and inhuman endeavor. And yet it is a finding of modern psychology that detachment is of primary importance for human development and must extend even into the subconscious and eliminate fixations acquired in earlier periods of life. As Erich Fromm points out, without detachment one can never cut completely one's umbilical cord to mother, father, family, race, state, status, money, and gods. One can never emerge fully as oneself. One can never be fully born.[6]

True contemplation entails detachment from our most basic need: the need to know, to reason, to have concepts and images. True contemplation especially demands detachment from our images and concepts of God. Because Christians find it difficult to detach themselves from these images and concepts, the words of St. John of the Cross are still relevant today: some people are retarded in their spiritual life and still think of God as

little children do, and speak of God as little children do, and feel
and experience God as little children do. Of course St. John is
not criticizing evangelical simplicity: he is complaining about
those who, when calling God a father, imagine characteristics of
an earthly father and retain the illusion of a fatherly God. This
is far different from the experience of true mystics who, when
they come face-to-face with God, encounter a wall of nothing-
ness, a night to the soul, and a void that is empty of all
thoughts and images.

Zen is invaluable to the above explained aspect of contemplative prayer which places the Christian in dark faith; Zen is
certainly helpful to the Christian who advances beyond the
stage in which God makes himself accessible to the mind in
simple images. And Zen reinforces in the contemplative the
knowledge of God which is not that of an object prayed to by a
subject. Let me explain this further.

In contemplative prayer, there is no knowledge of an object.
In his book on contemplative prayer, *Privy Council*, a four-
teenth-century English author cautions his reader, the contemplative, to forsake good thoughts as well as bad thoughts and
not to smother contemplative prayer with meditations and con-
ceptual thinking. He goes on to explain that at this stage in the
contemplative life of prayer, images form a barrier between the
soul and God and must therefore be forgotten. Nothing must
remain in the mind, not one creature. For the smallest crea-
turely idea is still as big as God because it keeps God out
entirely. "Be blind in this time," writes the author in his work
on contemplative prayer, *The Cloud of Unknowing*, and be
detached from even the holiest things that are not God.[7] This
kind of contemplative prayer is not rooted upon anything one
can think of or discern; instead it is founded on naked faith.

This rejection of creatures and thoughts includes for the
time not attending to the humanity of Christ, a creature created
in time and born of the Virgin Mary. True contemplative prayer
does not terminate at the human nature of Christ, of whom we
can have concepts, but at the person of Christ, who is the person of God. Even the human nature of Christ now risen and
coextensive with the universe escapes all the images and
thoughts we might possibly have of him.

This is why T. S. Eliot, describing the stillness and the darkness that is at the center of the contemplative's being, urges the contemplative to wait without hope or love or thought. Eliot explains that the contemplative is not ready for thought, and that for the contemplative, hope and love would be for the wrong object. The contemplative must abandon hope in, love for, and thought about creatures and seek instead the darkness of a faith enlightened by supernatural love.[8]

As I just mentioned, in contemplative prayer there is no knowledge of a subject. This does not mean that in prayer one destroys the self. As the author of the *The Cloud of Unknowing* claims, one cannot un-be, for that would be madness. Rather, one wishes to destroy the knowing and feeling of the self. According to Teilhard de Chardin, this destroying of knowing and feeling is the essential aspiration of all mysticism. To achieve this, one dismisses oneself simply as an isolated part and instead sees oneself as part of the whole. This is not self-annihilating pantheism. This agrees with the common teaching of the Church which holds that creation adds nothing to God or to the sum total of reality. Hence contemplatives strive to forget all essences and instead center their prayer on the only reality that really is. And when they see God as their own true being, they see their own real self, and in doing so they fulfill the Lord's Commandment: "Whoever loves me, let him forsake himself" (Matt. 16:24).

This traditional teaching of the Church does not mean that the contemplative loses his identity, rather it emphasizes that the contemplative's real identity is quite other than what it appears to be. Nor does this teaching deny a place for an I-Thou relationship between the contemplative and God. What the teaching does do is help the contemplative to relax his grip on anxious questions concerning the "I" and the "Thou" of the relationship. For to do less is to cling to the familiar self and its fulfillment; this lesser form of prayer, the Church teaches, can guarantee no fulfillment at all.

The point at issue here—our knowledge of our true self—is central to both Zen and Christian contemplation. Dom Aelred Graham, the Catholic Benedictine and author of *Zen Catholicism*, asserts that the chief source of our distress is that we identify our true selves with our assertive, separate egos, the often all-too-demanding "me" in each of us. This separate conscious ego sees itself as the center and interprets everything in terms of itself; thus it can block a direct contact with reality and union with God more effectively than vice.

So central is the issue of knowledge of the true self to contemplation that Thomas Merton explains original sin as a lack of this knowledge. While speaking of Eckhart and Zen, Merton writes:

> The tragedy is that our consciousness is totally alienated from this inmost ground of our identity. And in Christian mystical tradition, this inner split and alienation is the real meaning of original sin.[9]

Now if this inner split or duality between our true self and our conscious self is, according to our own mystical tradition, the meaning of original sin, then Merton suggests that paradise, self-knowledge, innocence, and purity of heart are a complete emptying of self. Merton warns that this purity of heart is not that of John Cassian—a distinct heart which is pure and therefore ready to receive a vision of God—but that of Eckhart, who suggests that our purity of heart is poverty so complete that there is not even a place for God. Simply reserving a place for God, as suggested by Cassian, is to maintain a duality. Unlike Cassian, Eckhart expresses a Zen-like equation of God to an infinite abyss with the true being of the self grounded in him. Only when there is no self left as a place in which God acts, only when God acts purely in himself, do we at last recover our true self, which in Zen terms is "no self," and in Christian terms is the Kingdom of God. Zen reminds us, as do Eckhart, Merton, and many other contemplatives, that the highest point of our Christian mysticism is reached not in the experience that I know God or that I love God—not in any I-Thou experience—but in the experience that God lives in us.

It is most especially in this immanent aspect of contemplative prayer that Zen can confirm and assist the contemplative. Zen gives us a method to put contemplation into practice. The Zen training *sesshin* does not allow the student to analyze or theorize about prayer. Instead it plunges him at the outset into the contemplative act in which there is no subject or object. The koan *mu* is not an object of meditation. Rather, by becoming *mu* in unthinking concentration, the retreatant is no longer aware of an "I" standing against a "Thou." He is aware only of *mu*. Comparing Christianity and Zen mysticism on this point Yamada Roshi gave us a Christian Japanese translation of Paul's letter to the Philippians. The phrase "Jesus emptied himself" reads "Jesus became *mu*." The roshi urged us to become not good Buddhists but good Christians, to become *mu* in imitation of Christ. A Zen *sesshin*, directed by an accomplished master, can help the Christian to achieve precisely this goal.

Very importantly, Zen reminds us that in our Christian tradition the risen Christ does not stand apart from us, objective to us, in heaven, even though many of our prayers use this form of imagery. The Zen Buddhists would paraphrase their own *Sutra* and say that only for the deluded is Christ a sentient being or concealed within sentient beings. For the wise and awakened a sentient being is Christ. Indeed the Zen Buddhists understand the complete joy we experience as Christ grows greater and greater, and the "I" less and less.

Finally, Zen reminds us that Christian contemplation is not a looking at Christ, or a following of Christ, but a transformation into Christ. The contemplative reaches fulfillment when his ego is lost and is replaced by the fullness of Christ. We all know that for Christ to come to fullness within the Christian, something must die. Christ himself taught us, "He that would save his life must lose it" (Matt. 10:39). There is no contemplation without a great death, and it is especially in this death to self that Christian and Zen contemplation come so close together. The questions posed by the Zen master led me to discover that the Zen method and discipline help us to negate our superficial ego and find our true self—the hidden and mysterious person in whom we subsist before the eyes of God. And finding our true selves before the eyes of God, we will discover in the end, with Augustine, that in reality there is only one Christ loving himself.

CHRISTIAN PREPARATION
FOR ZEN

There is much in the Christian tradition that can prepare us for a Zen experience. Of course, Christianity is like a big house with many rooms, and there is much there that does not relate directly to Zen at all. But there is an ancient and rich Christian tradition of contemplative prayer that does parallel Zen meditation. I am referring to the absolutely orthodox teaching of the Cappadocian Fathers (Basil, Gregory of Nyssa, Gregory of Nazianzan), as well as that of Meister Eckhart, the Rhineland Mystics, and the author of *The Cloud of Unknowing*.

What can we say about this orthodox tradition? Since it so teaches us, we can admit finally, that we do not know God. According to this tradition, all our words, images, metaphors, and dogmas break down before the mystery that grasps us. However, before the words and images break down, the Christian usually must travel a long road. That road consists of the catechism, family and school instruction, discursive meditation, philosophy and theology, precious poetry—all of which have a necessary place in the formation of an adult Christian. And often the wisdom we gather in our formative years is hard won and is well defended against doubt and cynicism.

But all these words and dogmatic statements are thoughts about God and emotions about God; they are not knowledge of God. Neither is the contemplative act knowledge of God. Instead it is the naked intent of the will reaching out to God as he is in himself, not as we imagine him to be or as he is in any of his works or gifts.

In a memorable phrase St. Basil explains that anyone who says he knows God is perverted. Not merely wrong-headed, but perverted. He is so completely turned around and off track that he is a danger to himself to and those he teaches.

Furthermore, in the contemplative act we do not love God as we love other persons or things in life. God is not an object that we can love because God is not an object at all. When we are commanded to love God, we are commanded to love what we cannot think about or know or imagine. Again, let me mention *The Cloud of Unknowing* which teaches:

> I forsake all that thing that I can think, and choose to my love that which I cannot think.[10]

This means each of us is to love God until our heart breaks. We are to love God for nothing but himself. And for this love we are to renounce all else and become so poor that we do not have even a God to love.

Hence, as we do not know God, we do not know God's will. We do know that we are to serve, forgive, and be compassionate to one another, but how practically we are to do these things is only revealed to us moment by moment as the circumstances of our lives evolve. Therefore, those religious leaders who claim to know God's will and who impose that will on others are to be forgiven rather than followed. What a mercy that Jesus forbade us to judge another man's servant.

Indeed, we do not know God's providence. Our instruments have not yet reached the edge of the universe nor have our minds grasped the principles that govern it. Our meaning, purpose, and destiny are hidden from us.

Furthermore, we cannot even say that God is good. To say this is to project our own ideas of goodness onto God, and that is always fatal to our faith. For indeed when a disaster occurs, we may be scandalized that a "good" God could allow it. With this mindset we may have good reason to question God's "human" goodness! We may be tempted to ask: What "good" human being would provide for the world the way God sometimes does?

Two years ago the United Nations declared that ten million children would die of starvation in the 1990s. The U.N. estimates indicate that the number of starving children now reaches 40,000 a day. This means that each day 40,000 mothers beg God for bread and water for their children and their prayers are not heard. Let those of us who are well-fed pause to grasp this terrible reality. Let us remember that Gregory of Nyssa wrote that all we can say of God is that God *is* and that God *is* for us. Let us be aware that our precious ideas of goodness are shattered before God's awful providence. All we can do is bow in darkness and confusion and say with the psalmist, "The judgments of Yahweh are true, righteous, every one" (Ps. 19:9).

It is sad that organized religion, which should open us to and prepare us for this awful mystery, is instead so fussily pedantic. It is equally sad that organized religion domesticates and dwarfs God to a controllable and lovable size. Influenced as we are by organized religion, it is no wonder that our prayers can become a boring struggle to preserve images and analogies that do not serve a mature experience of faith.

Let us go further. The orthodox tradition tells us that Christians cannot ever say that they have any independent existence of their own. As creatures, we share or participate in the existence of God. Creation adds nothing to the sum total of reality. We have no place to stand that is over or against God, no reality from which to barter or bargain. Rather, we are created moment by moment and live moment by moment by every word that comes from the mouth of God. This is not in disagreement with Buddhism, as it teaches that there is no dualism. The Father who is up in heaven apart from us on earth is sheer poetry. Does this not agree with the psalmist who has God say, "Do you really think I am like you?" (Ps. 50:21b).

Finally, since we have no independent existence of our own apart from God, we can have no true merit. When we have done all that is expected of us, we have done only what we were given the grace to do. If we are faithful to blood and death, we are still unprofitable servants. Merit, which conventional religion upholds, is a child's game; gratitude to God, which orthodox tradition upholds, is all that is left to us when we grow up.

TEMPER OF SPIRIT

In 1984 a group of Americans of the Christian faith and I toured the Holy Land. The tourist bus left Jericho and turned up the ancient road that led to Jerusalem; most of us were silent. We climbed slowly toward the Holy City along the road that Jesus surely traveled. We passed the Chapel of the Good Samaritan, and as darkness fell we all seemed lost in our own thoughts.

Suddenly our Israeli guide stood up in the bus and shouted: "Sing, you must sing. No one goes to Jerusalem except in song." And, so sing we did. We sang all the hymns we could remember, until we passed through the gates of the city. In singing, we fulfilled the words of the Talmud that one should not stand up to pray while in a state of sorrow, idleness, laughter, chatter, frivolity, or idle talk, but only in a state of joy.

Of course we must pray no matter what state we find ourselves in, but the wisdom of the Talmud suggests a middle path between sorrow and silliness and that is joy. Not unlike the wisdom of the Talmud the psalmist chants, "I will go to the altar of God, who gives joy" (Ps. 43:4).

Buddhists do not speak of joy as a basic temper of the spirit that is required for prayer. Instead, they say that we must come to meditation in a state of self-confidence. However, their concept of self-confidence as a necessary state for meditation is very much like the Talmud's suggestion of joy. The Zen master Hakuin typifies this attitude which encourages us to take responsibility for our own lives. He warns against religious teachers that lead us to grovel in self-pity and make excuses for our failures. The Zen spirit is one of self-reliance and self-confidence. What talent we have is enough to accomplish the work before us. In fact, what talent we have is all we are going to get. No one can sit for us. No one can come to save us.

Zen warns us to avoid becoming a torn-rice-bag-of-a-man who spills out his energy fruitlessly and then cries that he can do no better. This Zen spirit of self-confidence is close to what the poet Frances Yeats calls hope. To her hope is the power that deepens a sensitivity not yet dynamically focused; the power that sharpens our anticipated vision; the power that assuages our fear that all we look for has no reality.

We can easily surmise that joy and self-confidence are not separate states of mind. We can think of joy as attained power, and therefore bring the advice of the Talmudic and Buddhist teachers together. From both traditions we learn that when we come to our place of prayer or to our cushions for *zazen*, we are to be the bridegroom, or the strong woman of Scripture, or the champion about to run the race. We should sit and/or contemplate in joy and self-confidence.

PART II

QUICKSILVER

THE POETRY
OF INSPIRATION AND DESIRE

The flowering of a withered tree an eternal Spring.

Hunting a unicorn a man rode backwards

on a jade elephant.

Now he dwells alone beyond a thousand peaks,

Blessed with bright moonshine and pure breezes.

COLD MOUNTAIN

If you're looking for a place to rest,
Cold Mountain is good for a long stay.
The breeze blowing through the dark pines
sounds better the closer you come.
And under the trees a white haired man . . .
Ten years now he hasn't gone home;
he's even forgotten the road he came by.[1]

Cold Mountain is a real place. It is located in a range of mountains stretching along the sea coast of China, South of the Bay of Hangchow. But Cold Mountain is also the name of a man, a poor and eccentric poet, who, between the eighth and ninth centuries, lived on that mountain and sat with complete attention. His poetry continues to astonish us with its compelling religious feeling. Finally, Cold Mountain is a state of mind. It is the mystical process which embodies the hidden treasures of the Buddha who is not to be sought in a place outside ourselves, but in our mind.[2]

Let's consider other lines from the mystical poet of Cold Mountain which invite us to enter this state of mind:

Wonderful, this road to Cold Mountain—
Yet there's no sign of horse or carriage.[3]

and again:

Now it is that, straying from the path,
You ask your shadow, "which way from here?"[4]

As we can see, this "mystical" poet of Cold Mountain invites us to come and sit, to either begin or continue our journey along the signless road to self awareness.

In a compelling vision of a spiritual journey the poet invites us to join him:

> I climb the road to Cold Mountain,
> The road to Cold Mountain that never ends.
> The valleys are long and strewn with stones;
> The streams hard and bunched with thick grass.
> Moss is slippery, though no rain has fallen;
> Pines sigh, but it isn't the wind.
> Who can break from the snares of the world
> And sit with me among the white clouds?[5]

This invitation appeals to me for three reasons. First, the poet expresses himself so beautifully. Much of the world's Scripture is written in poetry. The *Mumonkan*, a book of koans, includes the works of Master Fuketsu who, similar to the Cold Mountain poet before him, used poetry to teach his students. Both the Cold Mountain poet and Master Fuketsu write in the poetic tradition of the Scripture. Fuketsu especially appeals to our sense of beauty when he writes:

> How fondly I remember Konan in March!
> The partridges are calling and the flowers are fragrant.[6]

Second, the Cold Mountain poet does not present himself as the traditional Zen master, deeply enlightened and permanently self-reliant. Instead, he expresses his feelings of loneliness, discouragement, and human weakness in his poems. He invites us to join his own spiritual search which is so completely human. We hear and touch his loneliness when he writes:

> I think of all the places I've been,
> Who would guess I'd end up under a pine tree,
> Clasping my knees in the whispering cold?[7]

We sympathize with his awareness of growing old with empty hands:

> Seasons pass and my hair grows ragged and
> gray; year's end finds me old and desolate.[8]

And we feel death pressing down upon him:

> The peach blossoms would like to stay
>   through the summer
> But the winds and moons hurry them on and
>   will not wait.[9]

How like us he is in his loneliness and desires. He sensitively reveals the poverty of those who are alone:

> In the wilderness, mountains and seas are
>   all right,
> But I wish I had a companion in my search for
>   the way.[10]

The third reason the poet's invitation to come and sit with him appeals to me is that he is a layman. The Cold Mountain poet lived when Chinese Zen was at its peak of creative activity and when many fervent Buddhists turned away from the formalism and ritualism of the clergy and chose to remain lay believers. The Cold Mountain poet has long been acknowledged and venerated in Japan as an example of an enlightened layman. The poet's invitation to us to come and sit with him differs from the self-reliant and authoritarian clergy masters. The poet appeals to us in humility, without hope of recompense or recognition:

> No one knows I am sitting here alone.
> A solitary moon shines in the cold spring.[11]

Now why would anyone who is not a Buddhist respond to this invitation to accompany an old hermit, to travel a never ending road, and to visit an empty place? The only reason for us to do so must spring from an inner affinity we feel with the poet and from our desire to share his journey of simplicity, humility, and loneliness. There is a certain type of temperament which not only naturally inclines itself toward silent and reverent attention, but also longs for it. Those who possess this temperament longingly seek the deepening silence and are drawn to the intuitive moment that shakes their universe. Such people eagerly accept the poet's invitation.

You may feel inclined to heed the Cold Mountain poet's call but may still question its validity for you. Why would someone from a theistic background, you may ask, want to sit with a Buddhist? Would any Christian not find the company of believers more congenial to his spirit?

It is true that the tenets of Buddhism and Christianity are poles apart, but the mindset and the spirit of contemplation of their practicioners are remarkably similar. In spite of the vast dogmatic differences that divide them, Buddhists and Christians who pray and are drawn to quiet contemplation often find themselves in agreement on the nature of their religious experience and on the values they hold in common: poverty, gratitude, non-violence, and peace. Buddhists and Christians whose personalities do not differ from the Cold Mountain poet's reach, out to inspire and comfort each other and to draw wisdom and refreshment from each other's spirit.

At the very least, theists will find companionship among like-minded men and women. They will find a friendship among those who associate with the Cold Mountain poet's spirit which they can not find in academic debate. Both the theists and the Buddhists who long for this simplicity of lifestyle and who realize the futility of finding it in intellectual circles, can use the poet's words to express their reality:

> I brewed potions in a vain search for life
>   everlasting,
> I read books, I sang songs of history,
> And today I've come home to Cold Mountain
> To pillow my head on the stream and wash my ears.[12]

PART III

SULPHUR

THE FIRE OF PRACTICE
AND TRANSFORMATION

Buddhas and living beings do not hinder one another.
The mountain is high and deep the water;
In the midst of contraries clear understanding
wins the day,
A myriad fresh flowers blooming
where the partridge calls.

GOOD INTENTIONS

When Tozan came to have an interview with Unmon, Unmon asked, "Where have you been recently?" "At Sado, master," Tozan replied, "Where did you stay during the last rainy season?" "At Hozu of Konan," replied Tozan. "When did you leave there?" "On the twenty-fifth of August," Tozan answered. Unmon explained "I give you sixty blows with my stick!" The next day Tozan came up again and asked the master, "Yesterday you gave me sixty blows with your stick, I don't know where my fault was." Unmon cried out, "You rice-bag! Have you been prowling about like that from Kosei to Konan?" At this Tozan was enlightened.[1]

Master Tozan was born in 910 A.D. at Hosho, an ancient city, long known as an academic center of Buddhist studies in northwestern China. Not satisfied with only an academic grasp of Buddhism, Tozan resolved to travel over a thousand miles to South China to study with the great master Unmon.

There is a great deal of human drama locked in this short intercourse between Unmon and Tozan. A young scholar finishes his studies and realizes he can never be satisfied with just an intellectual life. He resolves to leave family and attainment and to set out alone, in tenth-century China, to cross the whole continent, through many nations and across great rivers, to begin as a novice under a master he has only heard of. Surely there is nobility, courage, and tenacity here. And surely, Tozan must have thought that master Unmon would welcome him and appreciate his arduous journey and lofty idealism.

Unmon, however, was not in the business of appreciating idealistic young scholars. "Who are you? Where have you been? How long did you stay?" Behind these simple questions Unmon probes for attainment. Does this young pilgrim have any grasp of self, time, or place? Unmon realizes he does not. Tozan's answers reveal a mind that is naive and flat, lacking in any realization at all.

Anyone who has taken a step on a spiritual path will understand and grieve for this young man. I certainly do. After crossing America and the Pacific—in comfort, of course—and riding to Kamakura for my first Zen *sesshin*, I entered the room of Yamada Roshi; knelt before him, and looked up into his eyes. "Do you see anything?" he asked. His question reminded me of T. S. Eliot's

> Do you know nothing? Do you see nothing?
> Do you remember nothing? . . .
> Are you alive or not? Is there nothing in your head?[2]

"No, Roshi Sama, nothing," I replied. Silence filled the room. What a mercy for me Yamada Roshi was not Unmon who surely would have reached for his stick. "I understand," Yamada Roshi said softly, "I remember."

Let us return to the dialogue between Unmon and Tozan. After his first meeting with Unmon, Tozan felt humiliated and unappreciated. He returned to Unmon the next day to justify himself. "Why did you beat me. I can find no fault with my behavior." Unmon was known as a lion and his roar must have filled the whole temple. "You rice-bag-of-a-man. How long have you been wandering about like this, empty headed and looking for appreciation?" Fortunately for Tozan, Unmon's second arrow went deep. Tozan realized the content and impact of Unmon's words and became enlightened.

In my Catholic world I have often heard it said that God knows our good intentions. Zen would be silent on this point, but would suggest strongly that good intentions are not enough. It is not good enough to wander about from retreat to retreat, from teacher to teacher. It is not good enough to make sacrifices and set out on a spiritual path. Zen tells us that the journey must be seen through to the end.

What did Tozan see that turned him from a blind seeker and follower to a master in his own right? He finally grasped that all his going and returning took place nowhere but where he stood:

> Turning, turning—so many scrolls!
> Born here, dying there—nothing but chapters and
> phrases.[3]

Tozan realized that everything he sought was right there under his feet: he, himself, the world, everything was present and could not be otherwise. There was no more coming and going. The pilgrimage was over. The trick was done. Tozan's experience reminds us of the poet's magnificent insight:

> For years I suffered in snow and frost;
> Now I am startled at pussy willows falling.[4]

Suffering in frost and snow refers to childish reliance on others for approval, acceptance, affection, guidance, insight, or validation. There is a time of childhood for such dependence; the Zen spirit leads us to experience the reality to "be startled at pussy willows falling."

TESTING THE SPIRIT

Joshu came to a hermit and asked, "Are you in?" The hermit held up his fist. "The water is too shallow to anchor a vessel." said Joshu, and went away. He then came to another hermit and called out, "Are you in?" The hermit also held up his fist. Joshu's attitude toward the second hermit was very different. Instead of walking away, Joshu bowed to him and said: "You are free either to give or to take away, either to kill or to give life."[5]

Once when a Zen student was studying this koan he asked how Joshu could see into the true nature of the two hermits when each held up his fist in the same manner. How could Joshu approve of one hermit and disapprove of the other?

At this point I ask the reader *not* to try to probe the mind of Joshu, but simply to accept as fact that Joshu did indeed visit these hermits, did ask them to show him what they were doing, did decide how they were progressing in their practice, and did pass judgment on them. Believe that Joshu had a definite experience in life, and as a result he had a unique practice for his students to follow. He was the decisive judge of whether they accomplished the goal he set for them.

During a talk to his students in Kamakura, Yamada Roshi explained his own ability to judge his students, and his clarity and firmness on the subject resembled Joshu's. Yamada said that he had had an experience that we had not had, and that if we practiced as he directed us to, we might one day have that experience as well. The reader may find such a relationship between teacher and student extremely authoritarian and demanding. I believe that this Zen practice of the master's demanding relationship with his student offers a significant opportunity to those who wish to pray deeply.

Experienced direction in all religions helps the disciple. In my limited experience in the Catholic world, I have found that many Catholics reverence the idea of prayer and talk about it constantly. We have retreats, days of recollection, seminars, and sermons to discuss methods of prayer; we hold contemplatives in high regard. Despite this, we don't pray consistently and methodically, and we often feel confused and guilty for not praying as we should. Guilty though we may feel, our painful knowledge of former rigorous, and inexperienced directors, keep many of us from seeking out accomplished directors to ask for help. We fear that sort of demanding and authoritarian relationship.

If a not-too-determined Christian were to ask a Zen teacher to teach her to meditate, the conversation might go like this:

CHRISTIAN: Sensei, I hear you are skilled in meditation. I am interested in meditation and wonder if we could talk about it sometime?

ZEN TEACHER: Of course! Let us sit and meditate together.

CHRISTIAN: That would be wonderful. When can we do this?

ZEN TEACHER: Right now! Let's begin.

CHRISTIAN: Right now? But where?

ZEN TEACHER: Right here! On this cushion.

CHRISTIAN: Here? For how long?

ZEN TEACHER: All day, let's begin.

CHRISTIAN: Here? Now? All day? On this cushion?

ZEN TEACHER: Of course, you said that you were interested.

CHRISTIAN: Well, yes, but I hadn't planned to do it just now. I thought we could talk about it and I could hear about your experience.

ZEN TEACHER: Let's begin. Do it! Do it now!

To follow a Zen Master and to seek his direction, we must be ready, alert, and willing. This needed spirit of readiness to act immediately reminds me of a Japanese educator who once said that the purpose of education was to take a boy and pour some steel in his spine. I expected him to say to take a boy and pour some ideas into his head. This educator reminded me of the typical Zen teacher who is not interested in putting ideas into his or her student's head. Rather he would empty the student's head of theory, sit him on a cushion, and pour some steel into his spine.

The rules for practice in a Zen hall of meditation are exacting. For example, a student is expected to be in place on the cushion minutes before the meditation begins. During one retreat I attended in Japan, a visiting American Catholic Sister entered the hall a minute after the bell rang at four o'clock in the morning. The senior monk in charge of the hall looked up with complete astonishment. He leaped to his feet and picked up the stick which is used to rouse sleepy monks. With vigor he swung it at the Sister, just missing her and hitting the floor by her feet with a hard whack. The Sister turned and ran; the monk swung the stick again, just missing her and hitting the wall with another hard whack. As the fleeing Sister reached the door, the monk swung once more, just missing her and hitting the door frame, with a sound like a rifle shot. The Sister rushed barefoot out of the hall and into the snow.

Now, before the reader expresses outrage at this inhuman behavior, I should explain that the head monk had no intention of hitting or hurting his pilgrim guest. His behavior was an example of a dramatic teaching method used to startle and drive a point home—a point that was not lost on the Sister or on the rest of us, who during the rest of the retreat took care to arrive early all the time.

The highlight of a Zen retreat is the meeting with the teacher once or twice a day. At the sound of the bell, the student enters the teacher's room and kneels before his or her teacher, knee to knee, nose to nose, eye to eye. "Are you in?" the teacher may ask. "Are you asleep? What is happening? Where are you? What have you done since I saw you three hours ago? Give an account of yourself!" Like Joshu, the teacher learns about the student and gains insight into the nature of his spirit. Thus he is able to prod the student and test his or her spirit. One who is eager to learn welcomes the demanding challenge as well as the test.

THE ONE AND THE MANY

When all things return to the One, even gold loses its value. But when the One returns to all things, even the pebbles sparkle.[6]

We saw in a previous chapter that all forms are empty. When all things return to the One, even gold loses its value. The emptiness of all forms is absolute fullness. When the One returns to all things, even the pebbles sparkle—in other words, the Absolute is contained whole and entire in each fragment of the relative.

Consider the story of the old woman who sat by the road to Taizan below the mountain where Joshu was abbot. She was a wise woman who questioned Joshu's novices as they came and went. The novices were upset by the old woman and asked Joshu about her. Joshu told his novices he would go down the mountain and test the old lady. After a few brief words with her Joshu returned to his novices and told them he saw the old lady through and through.

Zen students sit pondering this story until they also see the old lady through and through. Does the Christian reader see through this old lady? Does the reader grasp the absolute whole and entire in the relative? Do the pebbles sparkle?

As Christians, we can be helped to understand this koan by much in our own tradition. Is not Christ contained whole and entire in each fragment of the Eucharistic bread? Is Christ divided in the Eucharist? Is he more here than there? Does the Christian see the Eucharistic bread through and through?

Listen to the words of Jesus: "I am telling you the truth: whoever receives anyone I send receives me also; and whoever receives me receives him who sent me" (John 13:21). When we receive another, when we give a cup of cold water to the least little one, we give it directly to Christ whole and complete. Do you see this least little one through and through? Do the pebbles sparkle?

Jesus said we would be judged by God on our vision of this very matter:

> Then the King will say . . . "I was hungry but you would not feed me, thirsty but you would not give me a drink; I was a stranger but you would not welcome me in your home, naked but you would not clothe me; I was sick and in prison but you would not take care of me"

> Then they will answer him, "When, Lord, did we ever see you hungry or thirsty or a stranger or naked or sick or in prison, and we would not help you?"

> The King will reply, "I tell you, whenever you refused to help one of these least unfortunate ones, you refused to help me" (Matt. 25:34–45).

And what is true of us in relation to Jesus, is true of Jesus in relation to his Father:

> Philip said to him, "Lord, show us the Father; that is all we need." Jesus answered, "For a long time I have been with you all; yet you do not know me, Philip? Whoever has seen me has seen the Father" (John 14:8).

The words "absolute in the relative" are so abstract. Christian tradition concretizes them in the ancient story of Marcellino. Marcellino was an orphaned child living with monks in a monastery far away. As the story goes, Jesus appeared to the little boy and held him in his arms. When the monks came upon this scene, they heard Jesus ask the little boy, "Marcellino, do you know who I am?" The little boy, with childlike faith, answered, "Yes."

Every Christian social enterprise, every school, every hospital, every soup kitchen, has been launched in an attempt to answer this question, "Do you know who I am?" When Mother Theresa took the first diseased and homeless beggar in her arms, she was answering "yes" to this question.

The spirit and practice of Zen can help the Christian answer this question upon which our salvation depends. Zen makes us take time, as much time as we need, to sit in silence and labor, until we see for ourselves the old lady on the road to Taizan through and through, until we can respond "yes" to the question of Jesus: "Do you know who I am?"

The practice of Zen may help the Christian see with her own eyes that all forms are empty, that all clinging and possessive love is a primordial delusion which brings terrible suffering. At the same time, the practice of Zen may help us to see with our own eyes that the One returns to all things, that the very pebbles sparkle, and that the answer to the question should be "yes."

For me, no one wrote more sensitively of the One returning to the many than C. S. Lewis. In one of his essays Lewis imagines that when we die and finally see God, we will not say:

> Lord, I could never have guessed how beautiful you are.
> We will not say that. Rather, we will say,
> So it was you all along.
> Everyone I ever loved, it was you.
> Everyone who ever loved me, it was you.
> Everything decent or fine that ever happened to me,
> everything that made me reach out and try to be better,
> it was you all along.[7]

THE SELF

The Emperor Wu of Liang asked Bodhidharma, "What is the
first principle of the sacred doctrine?" Bodhidharma answered,
"Vast emptiness with nothing sacred in it." The Emperor was
confused and asked again, "Who is it that stands before me?"
Bodhidharma replied, "I don't know."[8]

When Bodhidharma answered the king and told him he
did not know who he was, he was raising one of the most
fundamental, and to the Christian mind, one of the most difficult tenets of Buddhism, the teaching of no self or no soul.

There is an ancient Pali text that casts this Buddhist conviction in a dramatic form. A king once traveled far to meet a
renowned teacher to ask for instruction. The teacher asked the
king if he came on foot or by chariot.

"Teacher, I did not come all this way on foot. I came by
chariot."

"Your Majesty, please show me your chariot.

"Is the banner-staff the chariot?"

"No, Teacher."

"Is the axle the chariot?"

"No, Teacher."

"Is the seat the chariot?"

"No, Teacher."

"Are the wheels the chariot?"

"No, Teacher."

"Are the reins the chariot?"

"No, Teacher."

"Are all these things taken together, the banner-staff, the
axle, the seat, the wheels and the reins, are they the chariot?"

"No Teacher. These things are what they are."
"Your Majesty, is there anything else here besides the ban-
ner-staff, axle, seat, wheels and reins?"
"No Teacher, there is not."
"Then, Your Majesty, the word chariot is an empty sound.
you did not come by chariot at all."

In a classroom today, a teacher can ask a student if he
came to school in a car to help him see that the car—the wheels,
the axle, and the motor—is an accidental unity.

Similarly, a Buddhist thinks of a human being as an accidental unity. The specific contributions of Buddhism to religious
thought is that there is no self or soul at the center of our body,
feelings, perceptions, emotions, or acts of consciousness. There
is no entity within us distinct from our mental processes.
Though we habitually think of and speak of our inner self and
use words such as I, mine, myself, to describe it, the Buddhists
tell us that the self is not a fact, but rather, the result of our
imagination.

It is important to keep in mind that Buddhists are not saying that there is no eternal life and that the soul will cease
when the physical body dies. They are saying that there is no
soul now, that we are empty now of any inner core and do not
differ from a flame, a whirlpool, or a thunder cloud; nothing has
a life of its own.

I am what is around me.
Women understand this.
One is not Duchess
a hundred yards from a carriage.[9]

This central teaching of no self forms the traditional three
marks of Buddhism: suffering, impermanence, and soullessness.
We all suffer because we are coming apart, and we are coming
apart because we are soulless.

This Buddhist conviction is of course not unknown in the
West, as some of the poetry of A. E. Houseman illustrates:

I lay me down and slumber
And every morn revive.
Whose is the night-long breathing
That keeps a man alive?

When I was off to dreamland
And left my limbs forgot,
Who stayed at home to mind them,
And breathed when I did not?[10]

Or consider the words of Emily Dickinson:

Finding is the first Act
The second, loss,
Third, Expedition for
The "Golden Fleece"
Fourth, no Discovery
Fifth, no crew
Finally, no Golden Fleece
Jason — sham — too.[11]

Kathleen Raine sees that our "selves" are constituted by our relationships and expresses it most beautifully:

Yours is the face that the earth turns to me,
Continuous beyond its human features lie
The mountain forms that rest against the sky.
With your eyes, the reflecting rainbow, the sun's light
See me; forest and flowers, bird and beast
Know and hold me forever in the world's thought,
Creation's deep untroubled retrospect.

When your hand touches mine, it is the earth
That takes me—the deep grass,
And rocks and rivers; the green graves,
And children still unborn, and ancestors,
In love passed down from hand to hand from God.
Your love comes from the creation of the world,
From those paternal fingers, streaming through the
clouds
That break with light the surface of the sea.

Here, where I trace your body with my hand,
Love's presence has no end;
For these, your arms that hold me, are the worlds.
In us, the continents, clouds and oceans meet
Our arbitrary selves, extensive with the night
Lost, in the heart's worship, and the body's sleep.[12]

Though the teaching of soullessness is not unknown to Christians, it sounds to many of us like complete nihilism. We hear the words of Jesus: "What will we receive in exchange for our soul?" The soul is to be kept free from sin. The soul will return to God at death. We pray fervently, "Soul of Christ . . . save me."

Nonetheless, there are clear teachings of the Church and words of Scripture that can help us understand the "no self, no soul" insight of Buddhism. This understanding can add depth to our prayer. Teachers in the Church have never tired of saying that we have no independent existence of our own apart from God; we share or participate in the one reality of God. Creation adds nothing to the sum total of reality. There is no more reality after creation, but simply more beings who participate in this reality.

Jesus said only God is good. Here he seems to be saying that only God exists—with independent existence. Scripture tells us that Jesus emptied himself, poured his self out so that his whole life was turned to do the will of his Father. "Your Kingdom come," Jesus prayed, "your will be done." God was the "self" of Jesus, "I always do the will of him who sent me" (John 8:29). "For this I was born. For this I came into the world". Is this high virtue—or simply the way things are? Can Jesus' words help us to come to terms with the "no self, no soul" concept of Buddhism?

And what about us who follow Christ? Ibsen's Peer Gynt represents us when he asks: "Where is my true self that came from the hand of God?" We may imagine Jesus answering Peer Gynt, and through him us: "Your true self is found in every word that comes from the mouth of God." Our true self is given to us moment by moment. We live, we find ourselves, to the extent that moment by moment we turn to the will of God. And to the extent that we turn from the will of God to something else we have imagined, we cease to exist.

Would it not be helpful for us to bring something of the spirit of Bodhidharma into our prayers? Perhaps our constant prayer should be: Lord, I do not know who I am. I do not know the ground I am standing on. I do not know my true self that you save. I do not know what the whole resurrected Christ can possibly be. I repent of everything I have ever said or done. Your Kingdom come, your will be done.

If in prayer and in life, moment by moment, we turn from self preoccupation to the Kingdom of God, we will have the joy promised to those for whom Christ grows greater and greater, and the "self" less and less.

Listen to the Muslim mystic, Al-Bistami:

For thirty years God was my mirror,
now I am my own mirror.
What I was I no longer am, for "I"
and "God" are a denial of God's unity.
Since I no longer am, God is his own
mirror. He speaks with my tongue, and
have vanished.[14]

THE MIND

Taibai once asked Baso, "What is Buddha?" Baso answered,
"Mind is Buddha."[14]

When the disciple Taibai asked his master Baso what is
Buddha, he was asking about the experiential fact of
realization in Zen. When the Master Baso answered his disciple
and said mind is Buddha, he too was speaking of the experiential fact of realization in Zen. Neither disciple or master is talking about theories of knowledge. If the reader wishes to compare
theories of knowledge with Buddhists, the classroom is the place
for that discussion. Our purpose is to attempt to see what the
Buddhists mean by "mind," to appreciate their insight, and to
profit from it in our own Christian lives.

If there is no "self" and no "other," what is Buddha? When
asked this question, Zen masters through the centuries have
answered "mind is Buddha." Let us pause here for a moment.
Buddhists teach that the ultimate truth about reality—Buddha,
Buddha-nature, self-nature—is absolutely unknowable. We simply do not have the capacity to grasp it.

One day the Sixth Patriarch said to his monks, "I have
here something, which has no head and no tail, no name and no
attribute, no front and no back. Do any of you recognize it?" A
brilliant disciple stood up and said, "It is the original source of
all the Buddhas. . . ." The Sixth Patriarch turned on his disciple
with anger. "I said explicitly to you that it has no name and no
attribute; yet you still call it the 'original source.'" For good measure the Patriarch added that unless his brilliant disciple saw

this truth for himself, he could spend his life in a thatched hut and never be a true teacher of Buddhism.

Today, Buddhists believe that whatever the nature of ultimate reality (Buddha) is, its function is to see, perceive, hear, taste, smell, and imagine. They arrive at the conclusion that they are ultimate reality (what else could anyone be?) and they experience that this is how they function. They see, perceive, hear, taste, smell, and imagine. Therefore, they define ultimate reality (Buddha) by its function and say, "mind is Buddha."

Inevitably a student will ask, "What mind are we talking about?" the teacher will then ask the student, "How many minds do you have? Your own mind is the true mind. Your own Buddha is the true Buddha. One reality is all reality."

Buddhists experience mind as an everflowing stream which knows but cannot be known, something that is everywhere, but abides nowhere. The mind does not cling to the phenomenal world, nor does it cling to the void. It is utterly free. When this free mind, however, operates in human beings, when it is refracted through human nature, it appears divided. This is when we experience clinging and loss of freedom.

Another way of saying, "mind is Buddha," is to say, "everything is mind." By stating it this way, Buddhist thought can become more accessible to us. Emily Dickinson has explored this idea in the following poem:

The Outer — from the Inner
Derives its magnitude —
'Tis Duke, or Dwarf, according
As is the Central Mood.

The fine — unvarying Axis
That regulates the Wheel —
Though Spokes — spin — more conspicuous
And fling a dust — the while.

The Inner — paints the Outer —
The Brush without the Hand —
Its Picture publishes — precise —
As is the inner Brand —

On fine — Arterial Canvas —
A Cheek — perchance a Brow —
The Star's whole Secret — in the Lake —
Eyes were not meant to know.[15]

Everything is mind. The mind, the "Inner" in Dickinson's poem gives shape, color and meaning to the "Outer." There is no one objective world. Everyone lives in a unique world that contains everything. The mind is the "brush without the hand," painting the outer world and painting it precisely according to its own vision. This painting takes place on "fine arterial canvas." Outside the mind there is only the meaningless whirlwind; there is no Buddha.

Dickinson develops this insight in another poem on the mind:

The brain is wider than the sky,
For, put them side by side,
The one the other will include
With ease, and you beside.

The brain is deeper than the sea,
For, hold them blue to blue,
The one the other will absorb,
As sponges, buckets do.

The brain is just the weight of God,
For, lift them, pound for pound,
And they will differ, if they do,
As syllable from sound.[16]

It is not only Dickinson and other poets of the twentieth century that sing of the non-objectivity of the world. In the nineteenth century poets mused on the importance of the mind to the outer world. Percy Bysshe Shelley poured this awareness into a number of his poems. In "Mont Blanc," for example, he praises the magnificence of the mountain teaming with life and power yet concludes with:

And what were those, [Mont Blanc] and earth
and stars and sea
If to the human mind's imaginings
Silence and solitude were vacancy.[17]

The works of these poets can help the reader gain insight into the Zen belief of the subjectivity of knowledge and lead to the awareness that Zen's emphasis on the subjectivity of our knowledge coincides with the recent Christian emphasis on the subjectivity of revelation. In a more traditional reading of

Scripture, revelation does appear to be objective in its stress on the actions of persons, words, and events. But recently, Christians have begun to turn away from being solely preoccupied with the objective view, and toward an interest in the interplay of subject and object.

Much in modern thought is responsible for this change of viewpoint. Art, theoretical physics, and the social and behavioral sciences, all teach us how difficult it is to separate the observing subject from the object observed. We understand now more clearly than ever that the subject's involvement in every act of knowing exercises a prior influence on both the subject and the object. This insight suggests that the psychic structure of the individual is the prior framework influencing every contact with God.

Emphasizing the subjective aspect of revelation does not mean to understand faith only in terms of subjectivity, nor does it imply any severance from reality. Rather, it does insist that the social and psychological structures of an individual's life are the place where revelation occurs; they are the foundation for accepting revelation, and most exactly, they are revelation itself.

For Christians, too, the world is not a panorama of objects. It is a network of relationships centered on the person who creates and is created by his world. Hence a person is not a passive subject imposed upon by moments, events, and encounters; he is instead a subject who either limits or transcends every moment, event, and encounter in the uniqueness of his own consciousness. To help someone grow in consciousness, therefore, appears to me to be a most appropriate Christian endeavor.[18]

In their understanding and expression of mind, Buddhists and Christians may find areas of disagreement, but surely they are not strangers. Mind is the place where God reveals himself; mind is Buddha.

NO MIND

A monk once asked Master Nansen, "Is there any Dharma that has not yet been taught to the people? Nansen said, "Yes, there is." The monk asked, "What is the Dharma that has not been taught to the people?" Nansen said, "It is neither mind, nor Buddha, nor beings."[19]

One day years ago, when I wasn't even thinking of Zen but working through a pile of students' papers, I leaned back in my chair to stretch and looked up at the ceiling. At that moment I experienced what I thought I already knew, "everything is mind."

I jumped in the car and rode up to Yonkers to see Glassman Sensei.

Knock, knock.

Come in!

"Sensei!"

"Yes."

"Sensei, everything is mind!"

"Yes," said Sensei, "Yes, you see it.

"Wonderful. Everything is mind."

I was so pleased. I thought I had finally solved the Zen puzzle. Everything is mind.

Some months later I was back in the car again on my way up to Yonkers.

Knock, knock.

"Come in!"

"Sensei!"
"Yes."
"Sensei, everything is not mind."
"Yes," said Sensei, "yes, you see it."
"Wonderful. Everything is not mind."

I thought at that moment that if anyone heard my conversations with Sensei about mind, he would think it was Alice in
Wonderland talking to the mad queen. But I was grasping that
Zen is not about mind, nor Buddha, nor beings, but about *fact*
which is neither mind, nor Buddha, nor beings. Any *fact* shows
that mind is not separate from matter.

When the great Master Hakuin was a novice he had what
he thought was a profound insight. He went to his master and
announced that everything was mind. His master grasped
Hakuin by his nose and twisted it.

"Ow, ow, ow!" shouted Hakuin.

"Is this mind, you little twit?" said the master, giving the
nose of his bright novice an extra twist.

"Ow, ow, ow!" yelled Hakuin.

"Tell me now, is this mind?"

Fortunately, Glassman Sensei didn't twist my nose. As
always, he affirmed me and waited patiently for me to take the
next step. Even after saying that mind is Buddha, my next step
was to see that mind is not Buddha.

The steps a Zen student is asked to take are beautifully
explained in the following koan:

> The wind was flapping a temple flag. Two monks were arguing
> about it. One said the flag was moving; the other said the wind
> was moving. Arguing back and forth they could come to no
> agreement. The Sixth Patriarch said, "It is neither the wind
> nor the flag that is moving. It is your mind that is moving."
> The two monks were struck with awe.[20]

At first, I thought it was the flag that moved. Then I
thought it was the wind that moved the flag. Consequently my
sympathies were with the two monks who argued with such
great conviction. Hearing their confused dialogue, the Sixth
Patriarch had compassion for them and told them it was neither

flag nor wind, but their minds that were moving. Nothing—neither flag, wind, or anything else—exists outside the mind.

The Sixth Patriarch helped the monks take an essential step from object to mind, and hoped they would not stop there. The monks had to go then from mind to fact. Fact is life—it's what is happening.

Let us consider Kathleen Raine's poem "Question and Answer":

> That which is, being the only answer
> The question is its measure. Ask the flower
> And the question unfolds in eloquent petals about the center;
> Ask fire, and the rose bursts into flame and terror.
>
> Ask water, and the streams flow and dew falls;
> Shell's minute spiral wisdom forms in pools.
> Earth answers fields and gardens and the grave; birds rise
> Into the singing air that opens boundless skies.
>
> Womb knows the eternal union and its child,
> Heart the blood sacrifice of the wounded God.
> Death charts the terrible negative infinity,
> And with the sun rises perpetual day![21]

Raine points to flowers, fire, water, birds, sun, and death as fact, as the only answers.

In a similar way, the poet Louise Bogan wrote of her experience of love before and after marriage:

> What have I thought of love?
> I have said, "It is beauty and sorrow."
> I have thought that it would bring me lost delights,
>   and splendor
> As a wind out of old time . . .
>
> But there is only evening here,
> And the sound of the willows
> Now and again dipping their long oval leaves in
>   the water.[22]

The poet realizes love does not bring beauty, sorrow, or anything else. Instead she experiences the "fact" of love, like the sound of willows in the water. Every sound and every sight comes before every theory or definition. This is the dharma that has not yet been taught to the people. Beyond each fact as we experience it moment by moment there is nothing to communicate. Even if the stars walk backward there is nothing to communicate. Zen just sees. It explains nothing. Zen does not give us an absolute object, but it points us toward absolute seeing.

Once again Zen reminds us of something essential in Christian life but easily forgotten. Thomas Merton wrote that Christianity is much more than the intellectual acceptance of a religious message by a blind faith which never understands what the message means except in terms handed down by authority. For Merton, Christianity is above all a deep personal experience which is at once unique, but it is also shared by the whole Body of Christ.

Specifically, Merton explains that to fully hear the word of the cross is more than a simple assent to the teaching that Christ died for our sins. It means to be nailed to the cross with Christ so that the ego-self is no longer the principle of our deepest actions which now proceed from Christ living in us. It is central to Christian life to experience the fact of this self-emptying crucifixion with Christ.

In Buddhist terms, the fact of this self-emptying crucifixion with Christ is not mind. It is fact. It is death and resurrection now, moment by moment. This is the dharma not yet told to the people.

TEACHING

When Master Nangaku was at Hannyaji at Kozan, Baso stayed on the same mountain doing nothing but zazen day and night. One day Master Nangaku asked Baso, "Sir, what are you doing here?" "I am doing zazen," answered Baso. "What do you hope to accomplish by doing zazen?" asked Nangaku. "I am only trying to be a Buddha," replied Baso. Hearing this Nangaku picked up a brick and started to polish it. Baso was surprised at this and asked Nangaku, "Why are you polishing that brick?" Nangaku replied, "I am trying to polish this brick into a mirror." Baso asked again, "How can you polish a brick into a mirror?" Nangaku made his point, "How can you sit yourself into a Buddha?"[23]

An art teacher once told me that before even looking at the canvas he knew exactly what his student would paint. He knew the strength and limitations of each student and knew that each student would make the same mistakes over and over. Teaching individual students is much more demanding than lecturing to a large hall.

Zen teaching is done one-on-one over a long period of time. The teacher has time to learn the student's strength and limitations, and hopefully help the student not to repeatedly make the same mistakes.

Master Nangaku treated his student Baso with great skill. He saw this gifted young man sitting *zazen* fervently day and night and he led him to say with his own insight, "But you can't polish a brick into a mirror."

It is said that when the actress Rosalind Russell died, her family found that she had written in her prayer book: "Lord, give me wings to get to the point." Similarly, Nangaku labored to bring his zealous student to the point. "If you want to practice sitting or if you want to imitate the sitting Buddha, go somewhere else. But if you desire to practice Zen life then know that Zen has no fixed postures. The dharma, ultimate truth, abides everywhere and never abides in any one thing. To be attached to the sitting posture is to kill the truth within you."

A visitor to a Zen temple can usually recognize the beginning students at a glance. Their heads are perfectly shaved, their robes complete and in order, their sleeves folded just so, their hands held this way and not that way, their eyes cast down as they have been told. Hopefully before long they look up to see their teacher in front of them polishing a brick.

Zen is not another way of life. It is life itself as the individual lives it in her necessarily limited way. This mind that is confused and does not understand is the very mind of the Buddha. There is none other. Not infrequently those who feel threatened by life seek another way of living, structured, hierarchical, with robes and sleeves just so.

When I say that Zen is not another way of life, but rather it is life itself, I am reminded of what Thomas Mann says of analysis in *The Magic Mountain*, and I apply it to Zen. Zen here is seen:

> . . . as an instrument of enlightenment and civilization is good, in so far as it shatters absurd convictions, acts as a solvent upon natural prejudices, and undermines authority; good in other words in that it sets free, refines, humanizes, makes slaves ripe for freedom. But it is bad, very bad, in so far as it stands in the way of action, cannot shape the vital forces, maims life at its roots.[24]

When the monk Myo pursued the Sixth Patriarch to Daiyurei to take back the robe, the Sixth Patriarch laid the robe on a stone and said, "Take it." At this moment the monk Myo—like the young Baso—came to a most fundamental truth. He said, "I have come for the dharma, not for the robe. Please teach me." I believe these words should be written over the door of every religious institution: "I have come for the truth of myself, not for the robe. Give me wings to get to the point."

Because Zen is life itself, the teacher turns the student away from any answer to life. If the student stresses the absolute, the teacher reminds him of the relative. If the student speaks of the phenomenal, the teacher answers in terms of the noumenal. The teacher is aware that the student is often looking for an answer, a safe harbor, a package he can wrap up and take home and put on a closet shelf. And so if the student's theme is saintliness, the teacher stresses the secular; if secular, he stresses the saintliness. Always the teacher nudges the student away from the shallows into the middle of life.

Zen history gives a wonderful example of this teaching process in action. I mentioned that Master Baso helped his student Taibai realize that mind is Buddha. Taibai eventually parted from his master, withdrew into vast mountain forests and became a great teacher himself.

Years later Master Baso sent one of his monks to the mountain to find Taibai and test him. The monk asked Taibai, "What did you learn from Master Baso?" Taibai replied that Master Baso taught him that his very mind is Buddha and so he continues to live and teach. The monk said, "Master Baso has now changed his way of teaching. He now teaches that your very mind is not Buddha." Taibai replied, "When will that old man stop trying to confuse people? Let him teach what he wants. For me, this very mind is still Buddha."

When the monk returned to Master Baso and repeated Taibai's answer, the old master laughed with joy and said, "I see the great plum is ripe." (Taibai means great plum). In sticking to his original insight great plum was not being one-sided. Great master that he had become, he understood the point of Master Baso's test. Hence no matter how balanced a teacher is, he will always stress some insights that have shaped and are still congenial to his character.

I love this story of great plum because I have such empathy for his reply to Master Baso. No matter what I will ever realize in Zen, I will never forget that moment when a well-worn teaching became startlingly new: everything is mind.

In some ways, the history of Zen teachers nudging their students from safe harbors into the mainstream of life reminds me of Jesus. When Jesus called his disciples he said, "Put out into deep water and pay out your nets for a catch" (Luke 5:4). These words of Jesus are addressed to us today.

"Put out into deep water . . ."

"Thank you, Lord, for your invitation. I really appreciate it, but, you see, I'm a shallow water type of person. I enjoy the familiar, things close to home. I'm a creature of habit, I guess. But I'm grateful you thought of me."

"Put out into deep water . . ."

"Lord, you're not listening. I explained to you that deep water is not for me. You see, I tried it once, all young and idealistic, and it was awful. I can't take any more failure. Please ask someone else."

"Put out into deep water . . ."

"Stop it. Stop tormenting me. Don't you see I can't do it. I'm not good enough. Leave me alone."

"Put out into deep water . . ."

And so all great teachers of all traditions will not give us a packaged answer or an easeful harbor. They all remind us that:

> The way not to drown
> Is to swim far out
> And dive deep down.
> —Anonymous

APPROPRIATE TEACHING

> When Hung-jen, the Fifth Patriarch, met Hui-Neng, the Sixth
> Patriarch to be, he asked, "Where do you come from and what
> do you want?" Hui-Neng answered, "I am from the south, a
> commoner, and I have come here to become a Buddha." Hung-
> jen tested him, "How can a southerner and barbarian ever
> become a Buddha?" Hui-Neng answered, "The Buddha-nature
> knows of no south or north, no monk or barbarian!"[25]

I wrote previously about teaching and now I would like the
reader to consider the desirability of teaching in the language and culture that the student understands. Tradition has
it that Zen originated with the insights of Bodhidharma who
came to China from India. Behind this simple statement lie centuries of missionary effort of generations of monks and scholars
who sowed the seeds of Indian Buddhism in the language and
spirit of China. Since I played a brief part in the effort to make
Christianity take root in Japan, I am awed by the Indian
achievement. If Buddhism is Chinese today, it is because men
and women made it so.

But Buddhism did not only spring up in China; it took root
in Indonesia, southeast Asia, Tibet, Korea, and Japan; everywhere it adapted brilliantly and found a home in the new language and culture. Many of us Americans studied Zen in Japan
or with Japanese masters in America, and so when we think
Zen we tend to think Japan. But this should not be the case.
The Buddha-nature knows of no East or West.

Zen refuses to be identified with any specific culture and
refuses to imitate the style of any past achievement. While Zen

teaching maintains its basic Mahayana background, it expresses itself according to the art, poetry, culture, and insights of each country. The Japanese masters are the first to point out that this is so.

Yamada Roshi said repeatedly he did not wish us Christians to become Buddhists but to be as empty as Christ. And Maezumi Roshi told his successors in America that they were the ones to embody Zen in the language and spirit of America.

The mandate that is given to American teachers, to transmit the content while adapting the form, demands great sensitivity. It is hard to imagine two cultures more dissimilar than those of Japan and America. Someone once said that when an American greets a stranger he takes off his hat and stands up; a Japanese takes off his shoes and sits down. Japan is a floor culture. The Japanese are at home on mats and cushions and are comfortable executing profound bows. America is a chair culture. Americans are ill at ease on the floor, comfortable standing up straight, and uneasy bowing to anyone.

In light of this, American Zen teachers face a dilemma. They cannot just pick and choose those aspects of Japanese Zen that appeal to Americans, nor can they imprison Americans in forms foreign to their spirit. For example, suppose a native American Indian comes to an American teacher and asks help to see into his own nature. To see into his nature is the American Indian's birthright and the teacher must find skillful means to help him. And those skillful means surely need not include forcing the American Indian to master the exquisite subtleties of Japanese monastic life.

The American successors of Maezumi Roshi labor to Americanize the dharma they have received. Gempo Sensei tells his students that his Zen is not an "oriental trip." Joko Sensei explains Zen in terms of the American concerns with relationships, love, and friendship. Visitors to Glassman Sensei in Yonkers are startled to find not the quiet of a monastery garden, but a workhouse of social service providing jobs and homes for poverty-stricken minorities.

The ancient Chinese masters often said that the last word they wanted to hear from a student was "Buddha." In fact they told their students to kill the Buddha if they happened to see him. This was not a disrespectful attitude but a dramatic way of reminding the student that there is no "Buddha" but only the fresh fullness of life in each present moment. In the same respectful spirit we could extend the masters' teaching to say that they did not want their students to say "Buddhism" or "Japanese Buddhism" or "Zen Buddhism." To say even the word is to miss the reality. These questions are often debated. American teachers must proceed cautiously, but boldly. Those who ask for our help to see their own nature cannot wait.

Emily Dickinson understood that one truth can be celebrated in different ways:

Some keep the Sabbath going to church;
I keep it staying home,
With a bobolink for a chorister,
And an orchard for a dome.

Some keep the Sabbath in surplice;
I just wear my wings,
And instead of tolling the bell for church
Our little sexton sings.

God preaches, — a noted clergyman, —
And the sermon is never long;
So instead of getting to heaven at last,
I'm going all along![26]

Some years ago I had the privilege of visiting the caves of Ajanta, in India, where Buddhist monks lived and died in the nine centuries between 200 B.C.E. and 700 A.D. The caves are empty now, but they were once filled for nearly a thousand years with Buddhist meditation, study, community living, and precious art, and painting. But then social conditions changed amd the monks could no longer stay at Ajanta. Centuries of life lived according to certain forms and traditions had to be left behind. As I sat by the entrance to the caves, I thought of the freedom of the monks who marched off to embody Buddhism in forms that they could not imagine.

Surely the Christian community must look at the Zen attempt to separate spirit from letter with interest and understanding. Jesus himself had to answer similar questions from the leaders of his own religious culture. The Pharisees and chief priests often questioned Jesus when his disciples did not follow the letter of the law. On one occasion the Pharisees questioned Jesus:

> Why do your disciples break away from the tradition of the elders? They do not wash their hands when they eat food. And Jesus called the people to him and said, "Listen and understand. What goes into the mouth does not make a person unclean; it is what comes out of the mouth that makes a person unclean . . . For from the heart come evil intentions . . . These are the things that make us unclean. But to eat with unwashed hands does not make us unclean" (Matt. 15:12).

Sacred traditions and the culture in which they are expressed are "Not two, not one." They represent an ancient dilemma that never goes away.

MERIT

According to an ancient tradition, Bodhidharma arrived in South China from India in 527 A.D. and was immediately invited by Emperor Wu of Liang to visit him in his capital, Nanking. The Emperor, a devout Buddhist, asked, "Since I came to the throne, I have built countless temples, copied countless sutras, and given supplies to countless monks. Is there any merit in all this?" The Indian guest replied, "There is no merit at all. Although the shadow of merit may appear to exist, it is not real." The Emperor asked, "What then is true merit?" Bodhidharma answered, "True merit consists in the subtle comprehension of pure wisdom, whose substance is silent and void. But this kind of merit cannot be pursued according to the ways of the world."[27]

The story of the Emperor Wu reminds me of the story of a bossy old lady who died having accomplished much in her life. When she arrived at the gate of heaven the angel gate keeper asked her why she wanted to enter heaven. The lady replied, "I like to be where I'm needed." The angel was astonished and replied, "But you are not needed here."

The story of the bossy old lady makes us reflect and ponder. Imagine the angel going into detail: "Lady, you are not needed here. You are to be gifted here. You were not needed at your creation, but gifted. Your good works in life were not needed. You were gifted to share in the joy of God's creative act. All that you need do now in heaven, as before on earth, is to be aware and be grateful."

Merit is related to existence. If there is no true existence there can be no true merit. Only God is good. The rest of us are unprofitable servants. There is humor in the image of a creature before the creator, dressing himself up in "good works" and pleading his case for a reward.

Still we do plead and the list of our virtues is long. It goes like this: "I have built temples and copied Sutras. I have fasted and prayed, I have paid tithes. I have taught multitudes. I have delivered my body up to be burned. Indeed I am not like the rest of men. Now may I sit at your right hand?" For the Buddhists the answer to this question is stated clearly in the Diamond Sutra: There is no one to give merit, no one to receive it. In fact, there is no true merit at all; the shadow of merit may appear to exist, but it is not real at all.

For Christians, according to St. Augustine, there exists one answer to this combined statement and request: "I have been good; may I sit at your right hand?" Augustine tells us that everything is given. If we do any good work, we are given the grace to do it. If we call on God for help, we are given the grace to do that. Does not this Augustinian concept reflect the Buddhist's theory that the shadow of merit may appear to exist, but it is not real at all?

Much of our confusion on merit comes from our human vision. We find people who are good and love them. We should realize that God neither finds us good nor falls in love with us. Instead God makes us good with an unmerited gift. God doesn't need us, but rather lets us share in the joy of his creative act. All we need do is be aware and be grateful; these are God's unmerited gifts. God does not require any thanks from us. He wants us to be grace-filled men and women.

Our clinging to merit would be bad enough if all we asked in return was to sit at God's right hand. But we come to bargain and haggle. Recall the words of the brother of the prodigal son to his father: "I have slaved for you and you have never been so generous with me as you have with this other faithless son of yours." (Luke 15:29). Like the brother, we believe our fidelity should bring us good things in life. We ask God: "How could you let this tragedy happen to me when I have been so faithful? I deserve better. I merited more."

We are told that after centuries of frightful disappointment the Jews came to understand that there was no correlation between goodness and well being. They finally realized that God is to be loved until the heart breaks, and for no reward at all.

Another person who came to this realization is Penny Lernoux; she expressed it beautifully. Penny was an American living with her husband and daughter in Bogota, Columbia, and writing about the poor, abused, and homeless people in Latin America. She poured her energy, intellect, and compassion into her work for the unfortunate of this world and could well have thought she had accumulated her share of merit. But that was not her thinking. When struck suddenly with incurable cancer, Penny wrote to her friends:

> I feel I'm walking down a new path.
> It's not physical fear of death—
> Rather it is a sense of helplessness—
> that I, too, who always wanted to be
> a champion of the poor, must hold out
> my begging bowl; that I must learn—
> am learning—the ultimate powerlessness
> of Christ. It is a cleansing experience.
> So many things seem less important,
> or not at all, especially the ambitions.[28]

When Buddhists and Christians really pray, we figuratively come together at the begging bowl. As our awareness deepens, we know with Bodhidharma that merit is only the wisdom to know there is no merit, and that our stance in life must be gratitude, complete and forever. Perhaps then we will hear the words the Jewish scribe attributed to God: "Open your mouth wide and I will fill it."

IGNORANCE

Master Gasan of Tenryuji said, "I have accomplished everything in Zen. Only one more step remains: ten thousand sins." This koan reminds us that when Zen masters teach that there is no difference between good and evil, they are speaking in an absolute sense where there is no virtue or sin, no coming or going, no male or female. These same masters, however, recognize that in a relative sense there are human actions that spring from greed, arrogance, and ignorance. There are human actions, therefore, that masters such as Gasan would call sinful, although the term sin is used differently by Buddhists and by Christians.

However much Zen Buddhists might speak of sin, their primary concern is not so much with the sin itself as with its primary cause: ignorance. Zen does not speak of original sin, but of original ignorance. It strives to enlighten that darkness of mind from which sinful actions come. Not unlike modern therapeutic theory, Zen tries to heal the mind that has been abused or neglected, or so overly defended that it no longer perceives its original face.

I believe that one way to explain the Zen understanding of ignorance is to recall a Western classic that deals with ignorance and the tragic consequences it can have in our lives. The novel is Jane Austen's *Pride and Prejudice*. The heroine is a young woman, Elizabeth, who is bright, alert, and self confident. Yet in spite of her formidable gifts, Elizabeth at first misreads the reality right in front of her. Specifically, she misreads the character of one of her suitors, sharply rejects his proposal, and sends him packing. The young woman's mistake is understandable enough. Her suitor's character is complex and not at all like the young men of her neighborhood. We can sympathize with Elizabeth because we too have erred in our judgments of people, of events, and of the reality right in front of us. We have experienced falling into error by judging on insufficient data and on fixed expectations. We know how routine, repetition, and ritual can limit our vision. We also know through our experience that what is true for individuals is also true for large segments of society who, let us say in good faith, can participate in an absurd war.

The issue in question is not evil but ignorance. Elizabeth does not sin; she falls into error. Through no fault of her own she is ignorant of the nature of the reality right in front of her. But though Elizabeth is innocent, she suffers for her mistake. She almost loses a great house and a man who, she comes to understand, will be for her a perfect husband. The turning point in the novel occurs when Elizabeth realizes she has made a mistake. She looks at her suitor again, revises her judgment, and changes her mind. She looks at reality until she sees it as it really is. In brief, Elizabeth possesses the extraordinary capacity to change her mind; she has a consciousness not wholly dependent on what she was told or on what she thought before. The novel makes clear for the reader the education of her vision.

Not only modern literature, but modern psychoanalytic theory enforces the Zen preference for healing our ignorance of who we truly are. The British analyst W. W. Winnicott is most helpful here. Winnicott observes that an adequately nurtured child develops the strength and confidence to express its own needs and desires. But a less fortunate child can be seduced into compliance with environmental demands. Such a child may grow up to be just like the parent or whoever dominates the scene and may develop a false self that hides the person nature intended.

For children who have been sidetracked into compliance with others, moral education is not usually helpful. The compliant child knows in his bones that hope is locked up in his antisocial behavior and despair is linked with compliance and false socialization.

Literature and psychology are not talking about the same "true self" Zen is, but they can move us toward understanding

Zen's emphasis on the ignorance of the self that often causes our unhappiness as well as our problems.

There is a Zen koan that may sharpen our vision into the nature of our true self. Master Gutei, whenever he was questioned, just raised one finger. At one time he had a young attendant. When a visitor asked, "What is the Zen your master is teaching?" the boy also stuck up one finger. Hearing of this, Gutei cut off the boy's finger with a knife. As the boy ran out screaming with pain, Gutei called to him. When the boy turned his head, Gutei stuck up his finger. The boy was suddenly enlightened.

When Gutei was about to die, he said to the assembled monks, "I attained Tenryu's Zen of one finger. I used it all through my life, but could not exhaust it." When he had finished saying this, he died.

Perhaps the reader recoils from the image of a teacher cutting off a boy's finger for a childish mistake. But does not Gutei's dramatic action in this story remind us of the teaching of Jesus?

> So if your hand makes you lose your faith, cut it off! It is better for you to enter life without a hand than to keep both hands and go off to hell, to the fire that never goes out. And if your foot makes you lose your faith, cut it off! It is better for you to enter life without a foot than to keep both feet and be thrown into hell. And if your eye makes you lose your faith, take it out! It is better for you to enter the Kingdom of God with only one eye then to keep both eyes and be thrown into hell (Matt. 18:8–9).

But let us return to Gutei. When this master taught Zen by holding up one finger, he was expressing his lifetime of search, inner struggle, and attainment. Gutei's finger represented his having united in his own person the duality of subject and object. The finger is Gutei himself; it is the absolute that embraces the whole universe. No other Zen teacher has expressed himself in exactly this way—nor could he.

For the boy attendant, raising one finger meant none of the things that it meant for his master. The boy was simply imitating what he had seen and heard. Worse, he was imitating literally, as if the finger had some magic quality. There was nothing in the boy of search, struggle, or attainment. He had no insight that the finger—or the toe for that matter—was the absolute that embraced the whole universe. What a mercy that the master cut off the boy's finger—the finger of imitation. The boy lost his finger but found his own true self, his own vision, and the confidence to live it out in the world.

Christian spiritual writers frequently urge us to imitate the saints or founding fathers and mothers of religious orders; they also recommend that we embrace this or that spirit of the times. Zen, however, teaches us the vital importance of educating our own vision. There is no one to imitate, there is no time but now, there is no path but our own. It may not be sin at all that keeps us from self-awareness; it may be imitation and the pious repetition of routine and ritual that leave us ignorant of who we are.

> Your own road
> You shall follow it
> Your own truth
> You shall learn it
> Your own death
> You shall endure it[29]

On his deathbed Gutei told his monks that he practiced this Zen of one finger all his life and could not exhaust it. How could he exhaust it? We are exhausted by behavior that is repetitious and thoughts that are obsessive; the fact of life fresh before our eyes moment by moment never exhausts us.

IMITATION

A monk once wanted to ask Unmon a question and started to say, "The light serenely shines over the whole universe." Before he had even finished the first line, Unmon suddenly interrupted, "Isn't that the poem of someone else?" The monk answered, "Yes, it is." Unmon said, "You have missed it!" Later Master Shisen took up this koan and said, "Now tell me, why has this monk missed it?"[30]

We met Master Unmon earlier in this book when he gave the pilgrim Tozan sixty blows with his stick. Unmon is a towering giant among masters and his commentators praise him, in the Zen fashion, in seemingly critical terms. They have called Unmon absurd, an eternal clown who is always fiddling around. His critics say he is a cruel lion to his novices, too poor a host to offer a decent meal to his guests, and so vulgar that he props up the gate of Buddhism with a shit stick. Laughing at him, commentators say: "See how our house is decayed."

At first I found Unmon difficult; yet after working through the koans, I found that my deepest insights and my best balance have come from this strange teacher who loved playing the fool, but who also stood balanced on his two feet.

Let us look for a moment at Unmon's eager student who quoted someone else's insight. Know that this student monk had studied hard and had followed all the directions of his teacher. However when he tried to please his teacher by quoting for him an appropriate and venerable text, Unmon admonished

him. We can sense the student's frustration when Unmon told
him, "You've missed it." That's it. Take it or leave it. All the student's studying, pleasing, and quoting came to this. "You've
missed it." Today we must penetrate these brief words of
Unmon and grasp what the student of long ago did not. Why is
it wrong to quote another? Or more concisely, why is it so wrong
to imitate another? For a child, imitation is essential for
growth, but for a Zen student imitation will never bring him to
what is "missed." Why not? To begin with, we might say, if a
student imitates another's path, he will never find his own. This
is true enough, but such an answer would never have satisfied
Unmon. For Unmon the student must go deeper until he experiences insight for himself, once and for all. It is not merely a
truth that he should not imitate. The truth is that he literally
cannot imitate. In one moment of insight, the student will find
that all possibility of imitation will cease forever and he will be
firmly rooted in the emptiness of all phenomena, including the
self. There is nothing to imitate. Just as in the time of Unmon,
the student today is destined to be unique and free forever.

One reason students try to imitate is that they tend to see
ideals outside of themselves and try to achieve them. In
Thomas Hardy's last and greatest novel, *Jude the Obscure*,
Jude is a young man born into the laboring class in Victorian
England. He desires to go to a university and become educated. However, Jude does not realize that in his England of
the nineteenth century a university education is not possible
for a boy of his class and means, and so he pursues the impossible. There is a university in Christminster, the town next to
the town where Jude lives. The reader watches the young
Jude climb the hill near his town every evening. From here,
on a clear night, he can see the lights of Christminster faintly
reflected in the sky. The boy stands on the hill and dreams,
"some day . . . some day!"

Idealists and dreamers of all ages are prone to see some
ideal outside of themselves and try to imitate it. Many years
ago, when I first came to sit with Maezumi Roshi in Los
Angeles, I met with him in a private interview. In a moment of
what I thought was of great insight I said to him, "Of course.
You are Buddha!" Maezumi Roshi slapped me right across the

face. When I looked up at him in astonishment, Maezumi Roshi said to me: "You too!"

The reader might think that having experienced such a direct teaching method I would not have any trouble grasping the point of Unmon's teaching on the impossibility of imitation. And yet I did. Years later in Yonkers I continued to give Glassman Sensei moral and psychological reasons why I should not imitate, and Sensei kept pushing me to get to the point. One afternoon as I stood up to leave, Sensei said something that struck home. At the time, I actually thought the room tilted and that life would never possibly be the same again. Unless one continues to sit carefully, life can become the same again: habit, routine, and ritual can preempt what seems to have been an unforgettable insight. It is easy to again fall into the old habits of imitating and quoting others and pursuing ideals outside the self. If that should happen, hopefully one would hear Unmon, the old lion, roar: "You've missed it!"

Unmon's teaching finds a parallel in Christian thought. In spite of the classic text *The Imitation of Christ*, Christians are not taught to imitate Christ at all, but to be transformed into Christ. Christians are not urged to copy or repeat the words or gestures of Christ, but to have his mind and to be one with his spirit. Both Unmon and Christ encourage their disciples to act freely in the unique and unrepeatable moment by moment of their lives.

A Japanese poet expresses this Zen and Christian spirit most beautifully:

> There is nothing to be found,
>   even if I search.
> There is nothing to do
>   but to warm myself on my own.
> There is nothing to do
>   but to burn my own body
>   and light the place around me.
>   —Jukichi Yagi (1898–1927)

THEORIES

A monk once said to Baso, "Your Reverence, abandoning the four propositions and wiping out the hundred negations, please point out to me directly the meaning of Bodhidharma's coming from the West." Baso said, "I don't feel like explaining it to you today. Go and ask the head monk. The monk then went and asked the head monk." The head monk said, "I've got a headache today. Go and ask the cook." The monk asked the cook. The cook said, "I used to know the answer to that, but I've forgotten it. But I make good soup, would you like some?" "No," replied the monk and returned and told Baso what had taken place. Baso said, "The head monk's head is white. The cook's head is black."

This koan reminds me of an interesting Zen phrase called "sweeping the grasses." It refers to the young monks who went on pilgrimage to various monasteries to visit different masters for instruction. As they walked through remote places on their journeys they "swept the grasses" with their robes. When I first became a student of Zen, I went back to Japan on sabbatical and swept a lot of grass myself. My friend, Fr. William Johnston and I visited Kyoto to sit with masters and to meet teachers. I remember our walking all over Kyoto in the summer heat, sitting, traveling, reading, and asking "what is the meaning of Bodhidharma's coming from the West?" or simply, "What is the meaning of Buddhism?"

Let's return to the koan which unfolds in just such a setting. A visitor comes to Master Baso and asks him to show directly, without theories or propositions or negations, what is the meaning of Buddhism. Baso says he is too tired for instruction and suggests he ask the head monk. The visitor turns away from Baso (and from the very "direct pointing" he asked for) and goes to the head monk.

The head monk tells the visitor that he isn't well and is not up to instruction today and suggests that the visitor ask the cook. The visitor turns away from the head monk (and from the very "direct pointing" he asked for) and goes to the cook.

The cook says that the meaning of Buddhism is a very big question, that he knew the answer once, but over the years he has forgotten it. Now he just makes soup, but it is good soup. Would the visitor care to taste it? The visitor turns from the cook (and from the very "direct pointing" he asked for) and returns to Baso.

Baso asks the visitor, "Well, did you learn the meaning of Buddhism?" "No," said the visitor. "But your head monk is a sick man and your cook has stopped thinking. What a monastery!"

That night the three old friends sipped rice wine after dinner:

"Well," said the head monk, "Did your visitor learn the meaning of Buddhism?"

"I don't think so," said Baso. "He seemed disappointed with us."

"And he didn't taste the soup." said the cook.

"A pity," said the head monk. "All the way here on his sabbatical and he didn't learn anything."

"Perhaps next year," said Baso. "Besides, there is another teacher on sabbatical coming here tomorrow."

"To learn the meaning of Buddhism?" asked the head monk.

"Yes," said Baso. "I'll send him around to you."

"Maybe he'll taste my soup," said the cook.

Imagine! the visitor was in the living and breathing presence of Master Baso himself and he turned away looking for an "answer." The head monk revealed to the visitor the state of his mind and body, but the visitor turned away looking for an "answer." The cook offered the visitor a steaming bowl of delicious soup, but the visitor turned away looking for an "answer." I would laugh had I not done the same thing in Kyoto myself.

The preface to this koan offers a salutary meaning. "If you pursue someone's theory, how can freedom be yours? When the four mountains (birth, aging, sickness, and death) close in on you, how will your theories save you?"

The koan about Master Baso suggests to Christians that we give up sweeping the grasses looking for others to give us answers. The koan suggests that no one should ever bring an answer to a Zen teacher. Any answer we cherish and take home with us would limit and imprison us and make it impossible for us to act freely and creatively in response to new situations. The way is not in knowing answers.

In his introduction to *The Way of Chuang-Tzu*, Thomas Merton warns against reasoning about what cannot be understood and trying to attain what is never attained. He says that unless we learn to wait, watch, and grow without any appetite for self-improvement, we will destroy ourselves. Knowing and not knowing is the game played by those who sweep the grasses.

It is fundamental moreover, to keep in mind that if the truth of Zen is not in knowing the way, it is also not in doing the way. That is to say, the truth of Zen is not found just by living a good moral life. The Zen insight is not given as a reward for virtue nor is it taken away by sin. This does not mean that Zen is against virtue. The ethical teaching of Buddhism parallels the Christian commandments. But Zen is not primarily interested in producing well behaved and virtuous citizens. Zen is not interested in having us pursue good and avoid evil, nor in turning us into self-sacrificing people for others. There are enough moralists to do that. Zen opens our eyes to the good we now possess and earlier ignored.

I believe there is an example in English literature that can provide insight into this koan. In *The Ebony Tower*, John Fowles turns his artistic endeavors to the portrayal and dramatization of the theme of the good man whose ability to perceive and to act is circumscribed by theory.[31] In his story, David, a young English painter and art historian, takes a two day holiday to visit the aged well-known artist, Henry Breasley, in order to gather information for a critical introduction he is writing on Breasley's work. In brief, David travels to France to study the theory of someone else's art.

David envisions Henry as a giant of an artist who has long since left England and the influence of other artists. Hence

David's image of Henry is one of a super, self-contained, scholarly artist whose sole preoccupation is art. To his initial dismay David listens to Henry telling him in his assertive slang that he, Henry, is not a scholar, that he is ignorant of all the art history and theory that influence David. Henry informs David that far from being a theoretical man, he is a physical one, an "arty" man, living with two young women, not a third his age. One of these women, Henry tells David, is a student of art with promise; she has "the beginning of a hand." The old artist continues, "It is she who is doing everything a wife would do" for him: she keeps him young; she keeps his artistic self alive. Candidly, the old man tells David that he is very much aware of his reputation, that people call him, "an old rake and all that." And he assuringly explains that "he doesn't give a fart about" what people say and that he absolutely "can't" do without the young art student.

During his two day stay with the old artist and the two young women, David is dazzled, awed, and inspired by Breasley's achievement, his artistry, and his lifestyle. Perceiving this, the young woman artist, gifted with an authentic artistic imagination awakened in her by the old artist, invites David to share her imagination, her talent, her vision, and finally her bed. David considers her proposition, but thinks of his wife in England, of their very conventional lifestyle, and refuses the girl's generous offering. In so doing he knows he does the right and proper thing, but for the wrong reason. When he realizes this, his moment of transcendence with the young woman has passed, and with it her offering.

David realizes too late that his timid approach to sexuality does not even befit an adolescent. Simultaneously, he realizes the old man's secret: sin is a challenge to life. It is not an act of defiance or irrationality, it is an act of courage and imagination. Comparing Henry to himself, David concludes that the old man "sins" out of need and instinct and that he, David, does not sin, out of fear of punishment and retribution.

The trip to Henry Breasley's home forces David to confront reality and his alienated self. He sees that his timidity and fear of challenge diminish him and his talent. He realizes that his own painting is merely technically decent. He knows that his experience with the old artist and the young woman presented him with the choice to live and he refused. Hence he sees himself as he is, insipid and safe. With a despairing self-hatred he concludes that early in his life he killed all risk, refused all challenge, and so became an artificial man.

It is here that Fowles tells us that, different from the old artist who lets nothing stand between him and self-expression, and who wholly faces up to a constant recasting of himself, David constantly reviews his work in his "dutiful" conventional mind as he paints it. Fowles also points out that in the end, David knows that his failure is well beyond anything moral or sexual. It springs from his so-called urbanity, his love of being liked, his self-deception, and his blindness.

Fowles' last portrayal of David is that he is unable to grasp what the old artist and young woman hold out to him: the passion to live authentically. Our last view of David is in a hotel room in England. The visit with Breasley is over. Looking at himself in the mirror in Prufrockian fashion, David tells himself that he will not/cannot change, that he will go on painting as before, that he will forget this day. Later he will find reasons to interpret everything differently. He knows a scab will grow over the "wound of awakening," then fall away and leave the skin as if there had never been a wound. He knows he is an emotional cripple whose sole law in life is common sense. Consequently, in time, what he now sadly perceives to be a missed opportunity will seem to him the sensible decision, the decent thing to do. The young woman, whom he now feels he can't live without, will become just one more unpursued idea. And so he stands, staring blankly at his own reflection: he sees what he was born to be, is, and always will be: a decent man, an eternal also-ran.

I offer this critique of *The Ebony Tower* in order to help the Christian interested in Zen begin to wonder at the skill of Master Baso in the koan. By no means do I suggest that either John Fowles or Zen Buddhism is urging the Christian to abandon theory or to be unfaithful in marriage. Quite the opposite! Fowles criticizes David not for doing the right thing, but for doing it for the wrong reason. What the koan does reveal, however, is how gently but firmly Master Baso deals with travelers asking and writing about theories of Zen. He thrusts the fact of the dharma before them—and asks them to taste not the theory but the soup. This is precisely what Fowles' old artist asks of David.

SIGNS AND WONDERS

A monk once said to Master Sozan, "I am poor and destitute. I beg you, O Master, please help me and make me rich." Sozan said, "Venerable Seizei!" "Yes, Master," replied Seizei. Sozan remarked, "Having tested three cups of the best wine, do you still say that your lips are not yet moistened?"[32]

Zen training is dynamic. One aspect of it is called dharma combat, the public give and take, the parry and thrust between teacher and student or between teachers themselves. The purpose of dharma combat is to test and to deepen insight and to teach it to others. The two combatants on stage in our present koan are both capable.

Seizei says he is poor. He is not talking about money but he refers to his absolute condition of being neither a subject nor an object and he asks Sozan what he can do for one so poor. Seizei's question is his first taste of the best wine. Sozan calls out to Seizei and Seizei hears him. That is Seizei's second taste of the of the best wine. And finally Seizei responds, "Yes, master," this is his third taste of the best wine. Seizei, you are alive, questioning, listening, responding! How can you say you are poor with unmoistened lips. What other riches can you possibly expect?

Master Sozan clearly wins their dharma combat. He does not allow Seizei to negate everything, to remain in "poverty" with the emptiness of all things; rather he challenges Seizei to affirm everything, to see that he is not poor, that nothing is lacking to him in the dynamic world of eye, ear, and tongue. All Seizei has to do is open his eyes and ears, and riches will pour into him. He will search forever for something else.

I have been fortunate for many years because whenever I visit my sister on the Jersey shore I am able to watch the sunrise. I turn off the alarm, splash cold water on my face, and step outside to watch the show. From the first streaks of red in the black sky until the sun emerges out of the ocean, this show lasts for about an hour. I have observed that the sun does not rise one moment sooner because I am impatient, nor does it delay its journey for one moment because I am enjoying myself. In brief, I have observed that the sun does not care about me at all. When I pay any attention to nature, I observe her immense indifference to me. The Jewish Scriptures warn me about nature, of course: "Do the oceans ever speak to you a single word!" Still, there are moments when I feel ignored and look to nature for some response, but the only response is the moon turning its frosty wheel and "the sky [tolling] its grey dispassionate bell."[33]

Belden Lane, writing from a Reformed Protestant tradition, finds nature's indifference to us an important message. If spring speaks to us of resurrection, if November reminds us that all things pass, if the seasons and the elements teach us and console us, then surely nature's massive indifference to us must be a message we can read.[34]

I suggest that nature is teaching us that we are saved by that which ignores us, and that nature's indifference to our designs can be a source of our joy. Nature's disinterest in us mirrors God's disinterest in us that frees us from all our precious prayers and pieties. Nature's silence mirrors God's silence, and awakens silence in us. Nature's indifference to us brings us to awareness of God's indifference and refreshes our courage with the purity of his detachment. Does not our own experience of life suggest the truth that God is indifferent to our plans? How could we worship a God who paid any attention at all to our everlasting whining? It is not the purpose of God to glorify us. Is it not rather that we are made to glorify God, to pour ourselves out in darkness and silence, until the heart breaks? Is it not true that we are saved by that which ignores us?

To say that nature's indifference to us mirrors God's indifference to us and that God's indifference to us is salvific, does not call into question the Christian belief in the loving personal providence of God. It does remind us, however, that God's loving providence is a mystery taken on faith in Christian life and it does not always seem to relate to human experience. Even in our own personal experience we have had occasion to pray: "Lord, if you had been here, my brother would not have died" (John 11:22).

Finally, our human experience of grief teaches us that the laws of physics are God's laws and that God does not abrogate them to suit our fancy. Is it not wise to accept God's ordinary providence in our lives and not to feel "poor" and unloved, or to go looking for signs and wonders, miracles and cures, or manifestations of some extraordinary providence. Surely we are not a light to the Gentiles if we behave like disappointed and sulking children when God does not make the stars walk backward for us.

"What sign will you give us?" the crowd asked Jesus. Provoked to anger, Jesus turned on them and said, "This is a faithless generation and no sign will be given it but the sign of the prophet Jonah" (Matt. 12:40). Death and resurrection now. Take it or leave it.

Would Jesus not be pleased with the faith and teaching of Master Sozan? "Seizei, open your eyes and see the sun rise on the world. Open your ears and hear the waves break on the beach all night long. Open your heart to the cries of suffering men and women. How can you say you are poor and your lips are not yet moistened? What other riches can you possibly expect?"

If we take to heart this teaching of Master Sozan and Jesus, if we sit up straight and pay attention to God's world unfolding before us and within us, if we silence our selfish and ignorant petitions, then questions can begin to form in us. We will say to ourselves:

Who are you who watches this sunrise? Who are you who sits here and listens? Who is it who is coming to fulfillment slowly, in God's own time, not one moment too soon in spite of our impatience, not one moment too late in spite of our plans, until we can ask ourselves with the anonymous poet:

> I measure myself against a tall tree.
> I find that I am much taller,
> For I reach right up to the sun.

Slowly we begin to know that we are truly made anew each moment in the image of our silent and empty God.

HOLINESS

Attendant Kaku asked Tokusan, "Where did the holy ones of
the past go?" Tokusan answered, "What, what?"

The koan of Tokusan and his attendant Kaku is a corollary
of what we have seen before. For the Buddhist, there is no
independent existence or merit and consequently no independent holiness either. The Christian walks side by side with the
Buddhist on the issue of personal holiness and says with Jesus,
"Why do you call me good? Only God is good" (Matt. 12:17).

And yet, perhaps because of our sacramental life, some
Christians do speak of holy people, holy places, and holy times.
Some Christians speak of the holy as something made sacred
and set apart from secular use. Perhaps we could gain insight
into our use of language from the Buddhist experience.

The Attendant Kaku asks his master where the holy ones
go. Tokusan answers with just a "what?" Tokusan does not add,
"What are you talking about? What sort of a silly question is
this? Are you separating the holy from the not holy? And what
is this talk of going somewhere?" Mercifully, Tokusan does not
embarrass the pious attendant but turns aside the question
with a simple, "What?" The story does not tell us if Attendant
Kaku ever grasped the point. Indeed, even though this seems to
be a clear and straightforward teaching, Buddhist literature
provides many examples of monks who do not grasp the point.

A new arrival came before the great Master Joshu and said,
"I have come here empty-handed!" Joshu replied, "Lay it
down then!"[35]

In this koan Joshu urges the novice not to carry about his emptiness or holiness and not to turn what is really nothing into a
thing or a virtue. But the new arrival persists, "master, since I
have brought nothing with me, what can I lay down?" Master
Joshu—for the moment— gives up, "Then go on carrying it!" he
concludes.

This koan reminds us of Thomas Merton's teaching that
purity of heart does not mean a distinct heart that is pure and
ready for God. To prepare a holy place for God would be to separate us from God. Lay such holiness down! Only when there is
no pure or holy self left can God operate freely and sponta-
neously. In spite of this clear teaching from both the Buddhist
and Christian traditions, many insist on pursuing holiness,
emptiness, or something else apart from ordinary life.

Gilbert Murray asks the following questions: what accounts
in a human being for a loss of self-confidence, for a loss of hope
in this life and of faith in the normal human effort? What
accounts for a despair of patient inquiry, a cry for infallible revelation, an indifference to the welfare of so many suffering men
and women? And what accounts for a person's turning from this
world to "something else," to asceticism, to mysticism, to holiness? Murray answers his questions by saying that there is
nothing positive in this type of "holiness"; it is simply a failure
of nerve.[36]

Murray reminds us to be:

> careful always really to seek for truth and not for our own emo-
> tional satisfaction, careful not to neglect the real needs of men
> and women through basing our life on dreams; and remember-
> ing above all to walk gently in a world where the lights are dim
> and the very stars wander.[37]

Of course not every religious aspiration is born of pessimism
and failure nor does every religious enterprise try to separate
the holy from the profane. This koan is addressed to that
human condition—seen both in Buddhism and Christianity—
that does despair of everyday life and seeks solace in personal
holiness, in emotions, mysteries, and private revelations. Better
still, this koan is addressed to that part of everyone of us that
at least on occasion would turn from this vale of tears to seek
refuge in some "holy" place. It is for this reason that Glassman

Sensei does not use the Christian word "retreat" for the Zen week of intensive training called *sesshin*. *Sesshin* means to strengthen the spirit to live life with confidence and elegance. *Sesshin* stems our failure of nerve.

John Steinbeck, *The Grapes of Wrath,* catches the scent of holiness in the same way that Master Tokusan does. In the novel, Jim Casey is a preacher and a friend of the Joad family who tells Tom and Ma he would like to go with them on their long journey to the west:

> "An' you ain't gonna preach?" Tom asked. "I ain't gonna preach." "An' you ain't gonna baptize?" Ma asked. "I ain't gonna baptize. I'm gonna work in the fiel's, in the green fiel's, an' I'm gonna be near to folks. I ain't gonna try to teach 'am nothin'. I'm gonna try to learn. Gonna learn why the folks walks in the grass, gonna hear 'em talk, gonna hear 'em sing. Gonna listen to kids eatin' mush. Gonna hear husban' an' wife a-poundin' the mattress in the night. Gonna eat with 'em an' learn." His eyes were wet and shining. "Gonna lay in the grass open an' honest with anybody that'll have me! Gonna curs an' swear an' hear the poetry of folks talkin'. All that's holy, all that's what I didn' understan'. All them things is the good things."[38]

Margaret Miles of the Harvard Divinity School has discussed the original meaning of Christian holiness. She points out that before Christian faith was thought of as knowledge or commitment or community, it was lived as an orientation to the source of life; it was lived as a conversion to full vitality from the deadness of secular culture. Miles claims that being truly alive for the first Christians was not the opposite of physical death, but the opposite of death of the human heart: coldness, dullness, failure to respond, an obtuse spirit.[39]

Miles recalls that the meaning of holiness for St. Thomas was happiness: an integrated lifefulness that required the health of mind and body. Happiness for Thomas was the participation of the whole human being in the unique activity of God, which is love. For Thomas, happiness was experiencing God in the action of living lovingly by the delight of the mind and by the quickening and perfecting of the bodily senses. Miles assures us that a holy life for a Christian is one filled with the vigilance and energy necessary for effective relationships and lively prayer.

E. E. Cummings grasps the point of holiness as expressed in the literature of John Steinbeck and in the theology of Margaret Miles. Cummings sees human fulfillment in the courage to live and love now, not in some safe refuge:

> Suppose we could not love, dear.
> Imagine ourselves like living
> Neither nor dead.

And again,

> —let's then
> despise what is not courage my
> darling (for only Nobody knows
> where truth grows why
> birds fly and
> especially who the moon is.[40]

Perhaps here more than in writing about other koans, I must remind the reader that neither Steinbeck, Miles, nor Cummings are talking about Zen. I am using their artistic expressions to point the reader to the insight of Master Tokusan who would not tolerate the separation of holiness from life itself.

I believe that Master Tokusan would approve of the ancient Christian understanding of holiness that I have described. But if Christians would take a backward step from this world; if they would retreat to some other holier place; if they would experience any failure of nerve, old Tokusan would shout "What, what?"

LITURGY

One day when Master Unmon was speaking to his monks, the
bell rang for their next assignment. Dutifully the monks rose
to dress appropriately for the task to be done. Master Unmon
seized the occasion to deepen the monks' understanding.
"Look!" he said, "The world is vast and wide." He meant, "The
whole world is empty. You are empty. The sound of the bell is
empty. That robe you are putting on is empty; the task you are
going off to perform is empty. Why, then, are you putting on
this priest's robe when you hear the sound of the bell?"[41]

More specifically Master Unmon was saying: "Since you
are absolutely nothing else but what you see and hear,
why do you limit yourself to special or sacred times, places, and
vestments? Why do you allow restrictions of time and place to
impede your birthright of freedom? How do you move beyond the
opposition of self and bell?" Similarly, when I was studying with
Yamada Roshi he tested me one day in Kamakura: "Does the
sound of this bell go to your ear or does your ear go to this
sound? Show me. Now!"

Studying this koan, the student of Zen must not see objects
with his eyes or hear objects with his ears. He must no longer
function in the dualistic world of subject and object. Instead he
must live each moment completely at one with the specific task
to be performed. When the student does this, all he has left is
the seeing, the hearing, the putting on of a priest's robe, just the
doing of the task that the bell had called him to do. The Zen student must understand that this moment, this task, is the only

one in the whole universe. Thus he must experience it completely in all its uniqueness.

When the bell rings for the beginning of the liturgy, even though the world is vast and wide, even though all things being empty are absolutely the same, the Christian must live out completely the absolute difference of the moment. When one participates in the liturgy, one is not watching another's sacred dance; nor is one adding one's voice to others' pious song. Instead one is completely at one with the mind of Christ in death and resurrection.

How must a Christian celebrate the liturgy in a way that is conducive to being completely one with Christ in death and resurrection? How can those who wish to do so bring something of the Zen spirit to the celebration of the Eucharist? Many Christians who have experienced the Tea Ceremony in Japan have noticed the similarities between Tea and the Eucharist; some have tried to celebrate the Eucharist in the manner and form of the Tea Ceremony.

Although the religious dimension of the Tea Ceremony is inspired by Zen Buddhism, tea should not be considered a part of Zen Buddhism. Although tea is tea and Zen is Zen, the two are often intertwined. For several centuries Zen monks have participated in tea ceremonies, and tea masters have often practiced Zen. Consequently the Tea Ceremony is one way of experiencing Zen insight. The Tea Ceremony can also help Christians who wish to deepen their own contemplative spirit. There are actually six steps in the tea ceremony that can assist Christians in deepening their participation in the liturgy.

First, participants arrive early. Sitting prepares the mind and body to listen to what is said and to listen to what unfolds in front of us.

> Wonderful—the mood of this moment—
> distant, vast, known to me only![42]

Second, participants purify their mouths, hands, and minds. This is not the time to recount or regret our sins, but to let the sitting heal us so that we are one with not only those who celebrate with us, but with all the world.

> My father and mother in Paradise—
> Think of it

Today I go
To sit by their knees![43]

Third, the participant places something of beauty by the altar, something that makes the common fine, something that leads the participant to realize the beauty of ordinary things.

The three thousand worlds
... step forth
with the light snow . . .[44]

Fourth, in this moment of silence and attention, in this moment of purity and beauty, the participant hears the gospel proclaimed: Not too much at once that would flood the heart with words. Instead only a phrase or a word is often enough.

You want to know what's in my heart?
From the beginning, just this! Just this![45]

Fifth, service is at the heart of liturgy. The tea master is there to serve all. He folds the *fukusa*, his wiping cloth, into his belt, not unlike Jesus who, to wash his disciples' feet, took off his outer garment and tied a towel around his waist. And finally, the participants receive; they receive to the extent that they are aware. And what spirit is it that they receive?

At my house
These hundred plants
I planted and raised—
only to give them up
to the will of the wind[46]

The use of the form and beauty of the Tea Ceremony does not allow the participant to surrender to a narcissistic aestheticism. The tea ceremony is rather one human attempt for the participant to experience the immanent unnameable. In Catholicism, we can use it as skillful means to assist us to celebrate the death and resurrection of the Lord. Though the world is vast and wide, we are to live out the absolute difference of this moment completely. We all believe that the liturgy is a sacred banquet celebrated so that the Passover of the Lord is not just a memory, but that it remains forever present and living.

If you understand it, all things are one.
There is only one Christ, one priest, one liturgy

If you understand it, all things are quite different.
This liturgy is absolutely unique. It will never come again.[47]

So when the bell rings, even though the world is vast and empty,
have an answer for Master Unmon, and put on your robe.

PRAYER

The national teacher called to his attendant three times, and the attendant answered three times. The national teacher said, "I thought I was standing alone with my back to you, but now I find that you are standing alone with your back to me."

Never mind three times. Calling once and answering once is enough. The master's call is to show that he is alone in and with the whole universe. The attendant's "yes" shows that he knows that he too is alone in and with the whole universe. The calling and answering is the Buddha nature in disguise. The master is one with the calling so there is nothing else in the whole universe but the calling. When the attendant responds, "yes" there is nothing else in the whole universe but "yes." When each speaks, he is alone and the other is hidden behind his back.

I have chosen this koan to introduce prayer because of the extremely simple and total way that the master and his attendant speak. The master is Echu of Nanyo. He was held in the highest esteem in the Tang era in China and personally taught two emperors. He is best remembered, however, as the dharma successor to the Sixth Patriarch—honor enough for any Buddhist.

Echu had an extremely gentle and forthright personality. Someone once asked him what he had learned in all his years as a Zen student and master. Echu summoned a little child to him, caressed him and said, "If you are this, say you are this. If you are that, say you are that. Be as simple and unselfconscious as this little child." The practice of Zen is not just to see into our own nature. For some students insight comes easily and even mechanically. The true practice of Zen is the complete accomplishment of our whole nature. We are to live with the simplicity and unselfconsciousness of the little child Master Echu held in his arms. Is there anything sillier than students arguing over who has the better insight?

There are three incidents in the Jewish Scriptures that are excellent examples of a complete "yes" in prayer that would seem beneficial to anyone who prays.

First, God called, "Abraham," and the latter replied, "Here I am." This "Here I am," this "Yes" of Abraham is completely simple and straightforward. Old as Abraham is, he has the complete "yes" of a child. He does not offer an enthusiastic promise to do what might be beyond his ability. He does not promise a great and marvelous performance. He simply says I am here, all of me, and I am listening.

Second is the narrative of Abraham and Isaac in which Abraham is told by God to sacrifice his son. When Abraham arrived at the place God had pointed out to him, he bound his son and put him on the altar, then stretched out his hand and seized the knife to kill him. But the angel called to him, "Abraham," and he said, "Here I am," "Yes."

Abraham was sure he knew what God wanted, and he mustered all the power of his faith in order to obey. He overcame all his moral doubts and paternal emotions, he put aside the opinions of others and moved with conviction to the point of no return. But when called again, when new evidence presented itself, he stopped. "Here I am," "Yes."

What a salvific lesson this story offers for our prayer and our life. Abraham's example teaches us that we should never be so convinced, never go so far that we cannot stop, stand down, admit we are wrong, accept new evidence, or turn away from the satisfaction of perseverance. Without Abraham's ability to say "Yes, I am here, I am truly listening," our prayer is open to the fanaticism of needless sacrifice. One thinks of Joseph Conrad's *Lord Jim*. Lord Jim, in an effort to redeem himself, walks away from a living woman for marriage to a pitiless ideal. Conrad condemns him on every page.

"No," said the master.
"No?" replied the student. But yesterday you said, "Yes!"
"Yesterday was yes," said the master. "Today it's no!"

Finally, there is the incident of the boy Samuel in the Temple. Samuel thought he heard someone call his name. He went at once to the priest he served and the priest told him that the voice may be the Lord's and that if he heard his name again he should respond, "Speak, Lord, your servant is listening."

Imagine this sensitive child lying in bed in the silence of the night, listening for a voice that might be the Lord's. In those moments Samuel was listening completely. Listen with him; hear the Lord call "Samuel!" See this child leap out of bed. Feel his bare feet on the temple floor. See his eyes wide open staring into the darkness. Hear him say, "Speak, Lord," or "Yes! I am listening. I am completely here."

I believe this process of getting out of bed, of being in darkness with rapt attention and complete listening is a good description of *zazen*. And I also believe this process can add much to our prayer. Like Samuel, we have no idea of the mystery that calls us, no idea what the future may bring. We know how silly our words and promises are, how bankrupt our virtue. God asks that we be silent, that we listen closely, and that we say "yes."

The following anonymous poem expresses God's openness to the present moment that we are asked to share:

"My name is I am." He paused
I waited. He continued,
"When you live in the past,
with its mistakes and regrets,
it is hard. I am not there.
My name is not I was.

When you live in the future,
with its problems and fears,
it is hard. I am not there.
My name is not I will be.

When you live in this moment,
it is not hard. I am here.
My name is I am."

Let me conclude with a final example of this type of prayer with a story from the gospel of St. John. After his resurrection, Jesus appeared to his disciples by the Sea of Tiberias. He invited them to come and have breakfast of bread and fish. He spoke with them and encouraged them all. Simon Peter said nothing. He remembered that just recently he had said more than enough. He had "started calling curses down upon himself and swearing, 'I do not know the man'" (Matt. 26:74).

Peter might have thought that Jesus would never call his name again, but he listened and kept his mouth shut, and busied himself frying fish.

And then Jesus said: "Simon, son of John . . ." (John 21:15). Peter looked up. There were no more words now, no promises to die with him, no requests to sit at his right hand, no advice about not going up to Jerusalem. All that was now behind his back. Peter said, "Yes. . . ."

POVERTY

Attention! Jizo asked Hogen, "Where have you come from?"
"I pilgrimage aimlessly," replied Hogen.
"What is the matter of your pilgrimage?", asked Jizo.
"I don't know," replied Hogen.
"Not knowing is the most intimate," remarked Jizo.
At that Hogen experienced great enlightenment.

We have already considered the "not knowing" aspect of Zen. Now let us consider in this koan the radical poverty that not knowing brings with it. We are considering a pilgrim so poor that he lets go of knowing, having, possessing, and clinging.

In "Evaline," a short story in *Dubliners*, James Joyce writes about a young woman living in a dying city with her family and friends. One day she meets a sailor who is very kind, manly, and open-hearted. He has "his peaked cap pushed back on his head and his hair tumbled forward over a face of bronze." He tells her of distant countries, ships, of the Straits of Magellan, and stories of the terrible Patagonians. He also tells her that he has a home in Buenos Ayres and that he wants her to come and be his wife.

Evaline wants to go, to leave her home, and begin life anew in a distant, unknown country. And yet as she is about to leave her old life, which has wearied her unspeakably, Evaline does not find her old life wholly undesirable. She looks around the room, reviewing all its familiar objects which she has dusted once a week for so many years. Perhaps she convinces herself she will never again see those well worn possessions from which she has never dreamed of being divided. In her home she has shelter and food and; in addition she is surrounded by people she has known all her life. She wonders what they will say of her; will they call her a fool for running off with a fellow?

Evaline stands with the sailor among the swaying crowd at the dock. Through the wide doors of the sheds she catches a glimpse of the black mass of the boat lying beside the dock. The boat blows its long mournful whistle into the mist. Her resolution begins to slip away. Can she still draw back now after all he has done for her?

"Come," he says.

A bell clangs and all the seas of the world tumble about her heart.

"Come," he calls, and she feels him seize her hand.

No! She convinces herself she can't go. It is impossible. Her hands clutch the iron gate in frenzy. She sets her white face to him passive and helpless. Her eyes give him no sign of love or recognition. She lacks the poverty of spirit needed for pilgrimage. She can not give up clinging to her old possessions, not even to go to life.[48]

Mary Gordon wrote an interesting essay on Virginia Woolf, pointing out the qualities Woolf believed were necessary for one to be a good writer. According to Woolf, in order to write well a person has to write not of herself but of the characters she is creating in her story. That means writers should not project their own minds onto their characters. For example, if writers are angry, they might write in a rage where they should write calmly; they might write foolishly where they should write wisely; they might write of nothing else but themselves where they should let their characters speak their own voices.

Keeping these statements in mind, I would define poverty as purity of heart: the ability not to project the self onto the other. Jesus said the pure of heart will see God. Indeed the pure of heart—those who do not project—are the only ones who ever see anything. The others—who do project—see only themselves everywhere. They lack the purity of heart needed for pilgrimage; they lack the objectivity to be good writers.[49]

In her *Temporary Shelter*, a book of short stories by Mary Gordon, the author writes of "The Imagination of Disaster," that fear of life that can keep us from pilgrimage. For example in a story about a character named Billy, the main character becomes the victim of his mother's "truth" telling:

> I think that what she did was tell the truth to Billy, but too early and too much. The world is cruel, she told him, it is frightening, and it will hurt you. She told him this with every caress, with every word of praise and every spoon of medicine. And he believed her. Well, of course he would. She was telling the truth; she was his mother.[50]

People like Billy grow up to live pointless and unhappy lives. They are assaulted by failure and shame, by timidity and loss of love, by unhappy memories and bad dreams. Instead of venturing out on a pilgrimage, they seek shelter in love, loyalty, friendship, marriage, and the solace of the imagination. I am not suggesting that love and loyalty are the problem. Instead the problem is the fear of life that makes us seek love and loyalty as a form of shelter, a carpet to keep out the wind. In order to go on a pilgrimage, we must be so poor that we neither need and nor seek temporary shelter.

The Irish writer Edna O'Brien writes of the small land where she was born and of the provincial's insistent misapprehension of the larger world. She writes of unemployed men and of women with more responsibility than they can handle. Driven by fear of losing what little they have, they live parallel lives. By parallel lives O'Brien means that even in Ireland the Irish are forced outside the dominant British culture to form a subculture of their own with its own language and its own rewards. Even in America many Irish seek comfort in the sub-culture of the Church with its own language and its own rewards.

I mention O'Brien's work not to promote her view of Ireland, but to show my support of her view that that the fear of losing what little we have can tempt us to live parallel lives. Pilgrimage demands a poverty so complete that we have nothing to lose, a poverty so freeing that we can step out into the larger world.

The koan about Jizo and Hogen suggests that our pilgrimage through life demands of us a radical poverty. We are to be so poor that we do not know the matter of our pilgrimage, so poor that we have nothing to cling to, so poor that we have nothing to project on to others, so poor that we have no shelters in the storm, and so poor that we have no parallel life to escape to.

Finally this koan suggests another poverty that is most helpful for our pilgrimage—the poverty of those who not only have nothing, but have no one. Buddhism does not urge anyone to pilgrimage alone, but if anyone chooses to do so, or if anyone is forced by circumstances to be alone, then Buddhism supports their lifestyle.

Several years ago Joan Davidson, former chairperson of the New York State Council of the Arts, stressed the value of one who listens alone. She said that the artist, playwright, poet, and musician all look for the one in the audience who is prepared to listen. They look for the one who is not distracted by small talk or social demands. They look for the one who truly attends, listens, and experiences what is present before them, and then later is prepared to share what he listened to with others. Davidson did not mean, of course, that being alone guarantees that one is awake. Rather, I believe that her point of view is close to that of Buddhism which for centuries has taught that being alone can help some pilgrims be present to life, to listen to the dharma, and to deepen a silence out of which insight may come.

> "What is the matter of your pilgrimage?" asked Jizo.
> "I don't know," replied Hogen.
> "Not knowing is the most intimate," remarked Jizo.

The poverty of not clinging, not projecting, not finding shelter, and not seeking parallel lives, can lead us to the deepest intimacy of all.

CLINGING

When Bodhidharma left the Emperor Wu, he crossed the Yangtsu River and went to Mount Sung in Honan where he resided at Shao-ling Temple. This temple is better known as Shorinji. Tradition says Bodhidharma sat for years at Shorinji facing a wall. Some interpret the wall literally. Others take it to mean that Bodhidharma sat for years without distraction, that he sat seeing things clearly. What do the Buddhists mean by seeing things clearly?

The Zen master Rinzai in the ninth century taught four helpful ways of looking clearly at subjects and objects. First, he took away the subject and left the object. We talked about this when we discussed the Zen teaching which claims that beneath all our thoughts, emotions, feelings, and sensations, we are selfless, soulless. Second, Rinzai kept the subject and took away the object. He did this to ask us to grasp that the objects we see are as selfless as we, the subjects, are.

This selflessness of the subject and object is called emptiness. Emptiness means two things: first, there is no self or soul in the object or phenomena in front of us; and second, whatever we perceive is not a separate entity at all but one with every perception we have. All reality is produced by the interplay of cause and effect and as soon as the conditioning causes are exhausted, the effects vanish away. But we must not think there is something that will vanish away. Rather, at every moment, there is neither self nor other. The whole phenomenal world that delights or frightens us is wholly empty.

In his teaching, Rinzai is not asking us to accept the emptiness of all we perceive as truth, but to grasp it as a fact for ourselves, not to accept it at all; rather know it, taste it and live it. Years ago in Japan Yamada Roshi told us that the instant we grasp the truth of the emptiness of our universe, that is the instant our universe will totally collapse.

The last time I met with Yamada Roshi in Kamakura, I sensed it would be the last time I would ever see him. I asked him therefore to write a word that I could take home with me. Gracious as ever, Yamada Roshi assured me that he would and asked me what I would have him write. I thought of the phrase attributed to the sixth Patriarch, Hui-Neng: "fundamentally, not one thing exists." Tradition has it that one day young Hui-Neng saw an instruction written on the wall, "The mind is like a mirror. Wipe it every day. Allow no dust to cling." With this in mind, the young man himself wrote, "Fundamentally, not one thing exists. So where is the dust to cling?"

Yamada Roshi approved of my choice of words and the next day when I returned to Kamakura for my treasure, he presented me with his beautiful calligraphy. I carefully took it home, framed it to perfection, and today it hangs in my zendo, in solitary splendor. I never go in or out the zendo without bowing to Yamada Roshi and remembering his teaching.

Developing insight into the emptiness of the objective world, Zen teaches that clinging to this world, clinging to form, is primordial delusion. Clinging to forms that are empty is such a primitive mistake that it is not surprising that it brings humanity terrible suffering. According to Buddhist Scripture, all suffering springs from attachment; true joy arises from detachment. This noble truth so easily falls from the lips, yet it is a life long struggle to see things clearly and to free ourselves from deluded and possessive love.

The *Deukoroku* of Master Keizan probes our delusion with two poetic questions:

> Father and mother are not close to me;
> With whom am I most intimate?
> The Buddhas are not my Way;
> With what am I most intimate? [51]

Christians can profit from Bodhidharma's clear vision into the nature of things. Our own Scripture gives many examples of suffering that comes to us because of our too little insight and too much clinging. Remember the parable Jesus told of the rich fool? "There was once a rich man who had land which bore good crops. He began to think to himself, 'I don't have a place to keep all my crops. What can I do? This is what I will do,' he told himself; 'I will tear down my barns and build bigger ones, where I will store the grain and all my other goods. Then I will say to myself,' Lucky man! 'You have all the good things you need for many years. Take life easy, eat, drink, and enjoy yourself!' But God said to him, 'You fool! This very night you will have to give up your life; then who will get all these things you have kept for yourself?'" And Jesus concluded, "This is how it is with those who pile up riches for themselves but are not rich in God's sight" (Luke 12:16–21).

Remember the story of the rich young man? He had obeyed all the commandments and asked Jesus what else he needed to do to enter life. Jesus said to him, "If you want to be perfect, go and sell all you have and give the money to the poor and you will have riches in heaven; then come and follow me." When the young man heard this, he went away sad because he was very rich. Jesus invited him to fellowship and intimacy, but he was very rich. There were things he could not put down even for life itself (Luke 18:18–23).

Sometimes our things, our riches, are emotional. Remember the would-be disciple of Christ who approached Jesus and said: "Sir, first let me go back and bury my father." Jesus answered, "let the dead bury their own dead." Again, let us recall the young man who told Jesus: "I will follow you, sir; but first let me go and say good-bye to my family." Jesus said to him, "Anyone who starts to plow and then keeps looking back is of no use for the Kingdom of God" (Luke 9:59–60, 61–62).

Finally, at times our clinging to things leads us into the darkest night. "Then Judas, one of the twelve Apostles, a patriarch, went to the enemies of Jesus and asked, What will you give me if I betray Jesus to you?" (Matt. 26:14–15). They counted out thirty silver coins. Judas was a shrewd man and he knew the value of money. He would not have betrayed Jesus for twenty silver coins. But thirty? Yes, Judas would betray Jesus for thirty silver coins.

The British poet Stephen Spender highlights this tragic bargain when he writes:

The eyes of twenty centuries pursue me . . .
I stretch my hand across the white table into the
   dish
But not to dip the bread.[52]

The only thing shrewdness teaches us is how to be shrewd. Would Bodhidharma's clear vision into the nature of things not help us to see that? Matthew Arnold approaches this vision in poem "Dover Beach":

. . . The world which seems to be before us like a
land of dreams so beautiful, so new
hath really neither joy, nor love
nor help for pain . . .[53]

The practice of Zen may help us see that the words of Jesus, which at first sound so terrible, are in fact merciful and liberating: "Whoever comes to me cannot be my disciple unless he loves me more than he loves his father and his mother, his wife and his children, his brothers and his sisters, and himself as well" (Luke. 14:26). And again, "Foxes have holes, and birds have nests, but the Son of Man has no place to lie down and rest" (Luke 9:58).

CONVENTIONAL WISDOM

> Master Gettan said to a monk: "Keichu made a cart whose wheels had a hundred spokes. Take both front and rear parts away and remove the axle: then what will it be?"[54]

What will it be if you take the steering wheel off your car? Or better, what will it be if you take the rudder off your boat? Surely this is madness! To take the rudder off your boat is to drift helplessly. To pull up the anchor without fixing the rudder is to be criminally negligent. The meaning of the koan is not in its literal reading.

So what is the message of Keichu and his carts? Chögyam Trungpa Rinpoche writes of compassion as environmental generosity, without direction, without the "for me" and without the "for them." Compassion does not regard anything as being accepted or rejected, it just meets each situation as it is, sees it for what it is, and acts appropriately. Compassion accepts the whole situation of life as it is, the light and the dark, the good and the bad, the true and, yes, what seems to be false.

What compassion does not do is to rely completely on the rudder, or as the world calls it, conventional wisdom, for security. If we direct our lives to the light and avoid the dark, if we steer to the good and turn from the bad, if we say yes to the truth and no to what seems to be false, then we choose the hero's way. The way of the hero is the way of light, goodness, and truth, but this hero may be one sided, conventional; he may over-direct his life from a limited point of view that lacks compassion and environmental generosity. He may rely too completely on the rudder.

Wallace Stevens has written beautifully on the dangers of the hero's path and of an over-directed life:

It was when I said
"There is no such thing as the truth,"
That the grapes seemed fatter,
The fox ran out of his hole.

You . . . you said,
"There are many truths,
But they are not parts of a truth."
Then the tree, at night, began to change.
We were two figures in a wood.
We said we stood alone.

It was when I said,
"Words are not forms of a single word.
In the sum of the parts, there are only parts.
The world must be measured by the eye."

It was when you said,
"The idols have seen lots of poverty,
Snakes and gold and lice,
But not the truth";
It was at that time, that the silence was largest

And longest, the night was roundest,
The fragrance of the autumn warmest,
Closest and strongest.[55]

I believe Stevens suggests that though all truths may be united in God, we do not see that unity. To insist on one truth that we do see is to block other truths from coming into focus. There are many truths in every human being, but to steer toward one truth can block our undeveloped side from rising forever. If we grasp the rudder too tightly, we become predictable and repetitious, flat characters in a play who only read one line.

If we remove—relax—the rudder of the judgmental mind, then the fox runs out of his hole, the tree at night begins to change, and the fragrance of autumn is warmest. . . . There are many truths; we have not the complete truth, not the truth about God, our neighbors, or ourselves. If we had, we would have nothing to learn and life would be completely static.

Novelists warn us, of course, that there is danger in relaxing our grip on the rudder of our conventional judgmental mind. In *Damage*, Josephine Hart writes:

> Our sanity depends essentially on a narrowness of vision—the ability to select the elements vital to survival, while ignoring the great truths. So the individual lives his daily life, without due attention to the fact that he has no guarantee of tomorrow. He hides from himself the knowledge that his life is a unique experience, which will end in the grave; that at every second, lives as unique as his start and end. This blindness allows a pattern of living to hand itself on, and few who challenge this pattern survive. With good reason. All the laws of life and society would seem irrelevant, if each man concentrated daily on the reality of his own death.[56]

Similarly, John Fowles in *The French Lieutenant's Woman*, presents us with Charles, a Victorian young man who is in the opening of the novel caught by forces without and within that have alienated him from his true self. When we first meet him we find that he has learned to survive by blending in with his surroundings and by embedding himself in the unquestioned assumptions of his age and social caste. And so, in the vital matter of choosing a woman to share his life, Charles does the most conventional and obvious thing. He proposes to a pretty young heiress, demure and shy, monotonous and without character.

Charles's awareness of what he has become is ignited by his chance meeting with Sarah, a magus-like young woman; under her tutelage he grows quickly in self-knowledge and in the understanding of his world.

Breaking off his conventional engagement, Charles realizes all that is at stake for a new man to arise in him. All his years of thought, speculation, and self-knowledge, plus his whole past, the best of his past self are the price he is asked to pay. All that he ever wanted to be now seems worthless to him: "all lay razed: all principle, all future, all faith, all honorable intent."[57] But he survives, though infinitely isolated, with the righteous staring at him mournfully, implacably.

Charles gains a curious sort of self-respect in his nothing-
ness. He gains a sense that choosing to be nothing—to have
nothing—is the last saving grace of a gentleman, his last freedom. So severe is the struggle to grow beyond the rudder of conventional wisdom that Fowles intrudes in the novel and quotes
Tennyson's *Maud* to describe Charles's aspiration:

> And ah for a man to arise in me
> that the man I am may cease to be.[58]

The struggle of Charles to become free reminds me of the
dialogue between Jesus and Nicodemus. Jesus said to Nicodemus, "I am telling you the truth; no one can see the Kingdom
of God unless he is born again." "How can a grown man be born
again?" Nicodemus asked. "He certainly cannot enter his
mother's womb and be born a second time! . . . "Jesus answered,
"You are a great teacher in Israel, and you don't know this?"
(John 3:9).

The conventional wisdom of this world is folly, and the
Christian response to it is death and rebirth now. I believe
Master Gettan would approve of the teaching of Jesus. Let us
listen to Gettan as he challenges anew today from his own culture: "Take the wheel off your cart—take the rudder off your
ship—and what will it be?"

CHRIST

If you see the Buddha, kill him.

It is time to recall Thomas Merton's remark that it is a very complex and frustrating task to try to conciliate Zen insights with Christian doctrine. Nowhere is his insight more true then in dealing with the Buddhist saying: "If you see the Buddha, kill him." For Zen Buddhists, the historical life of the man Gotama is not of primary importance. If he never lived at all, the self confidence of accomplished Zen practitioners would not be shaken. They have their own experience, they see for themselves, and everyone else, including Gotama, is "extra."

As the Sixth Patriarch said:

Your mind is deluded and you cannot see, so you go and ask a teacher to show you the way. You must awaken with your own mind and see for yourself, and you must practice with the Dharma. Because you yourself are deluded and you do not see your own mind, you come asking me whether I see or not. Even if I see for myself, I cannot take the place of your delusion; even if you see for yourself, you cannot take the place of my delusion. Why don't you practice for yourself and then ask me whether I see or not.[59]

The Christian experience of the historical Jesus differs from the Buddhist experience of Gotama. One theologian expresses the tradition succinctly:

In Christian experience, Jesus is Lord, the mediator of God's saving power, the incarnation of God's love, power, and wisdom in the world. God has so taken possession of this one concrete human life that in it and through it (God) acts effectively and definitively for the eternal welfare of the whole human race.[60]

In spite of the dogmatic difference between the Buddhist faith in Gotama and the Christian faith in Jesus, I believe Christians can learn from the Buddhist experience.

Let us listen again to the Sixth Patriarch. He warns us that if we do not seek the "true self" and seek the Buddha outside of ourselves, all our seeking will be done in ignorance.

Deluded, a Buddha is an individual being;
Awakened, an individual being is a Buddha.
Ignorant, a Buddha is an individual being;
With wisdom, an individual being is a Buddha.
If the mind is warped, a Buddha is an individual being;
If the mind is impartial, an individual being is a Buddha.
When once a warped mind is produced,
Buddha is concealed within the individual being.
If for one instant of thought we become impartial,
Then individual beings are themselves Buddha.
In our own mind itself a Buddha exists,
Our own Buddha is the true Buddha.
If we do not have in ourselves the Buddha mind,
Then where are we to seek Buddha?[61]

"From the outset our nature is pure," says the Sixth Patriarch, and if we see this nature then we do not abide either inside or outside; we are free to come or go. Readily we cast aside the mind that clings to things, and there is no obstruction to our passage. Does not this teaching of the Patriarch correspond with much of our own Christology? If we agree with Augustine that there is only one Christ loving himself, then cannot we also say that for the deluded, Christ is an individual being, and for the awakened, an individual being is Christ. The risen Christ is not another being somewhere else, but rather the risen Christ is the being right in front of me, the same Christ that I am.

Teilhard de Chardin takes up this same theme in *The Divine Milieu:*

In a real sense only one man will be saved: Christ, the head and living summary of humanity. Each one of the elect is called to see God face to face. But his act of vision will be vitally inseparable from the elevating and illuminating action of Christ. In heaven we ourselves shall contemplate God, but, as it were, through the eyes of Christ.[62]

Could Christians not sit and learn at the feet of a teacher such as the Sixth Patriarch? Would not Jesus embrace a teacher who, unlike his own disciples, does not promise virtue, does not beg for favors and does not separate himself from the least of his brothers and sisters?

Recall Jesus' response to the Centurion's profession of faith:

When Jesus heard this, he was surprised and said to the people following him, "I tell you, I have never found anyone in Israel with faith like this" (Matt. 8:10).

In his next sentence Jesus seems to be including the Sixth Patriarch in his belief of who will make up the Kingdom of heaven:

I assure you that many will come from the east and the west and sit down with Abraham . . . at the feast in the Kingdom of heaven (Matt. 8:11).

There is a practical conclusion that follows from seeing that there is only one Christ. The reader may say, I need not imagine myself kneeling before Christ. I need not pray for salvation, I need not ask for virtue or for anything else as if it were not already given. The spirit of Jesus is fully poured into my heart. With all my limitations, I am Jesus in this world. I have been given all that I need to live out the spirit of Jesus in all the circumstances of my life. Salvation is given here and now. I am not to let any gap open up between Jesus and "me." How can I let any gap open between Jesus and me if I share the experience of St. Paul: "I live, now not I, but Christ lives in me."

In the seventh chapter of the *Mumonkan*, the author says that if a monk does not grasp the fact that every action is the manifestation of his essential nature, he will mistake a pot for a bell. If he does not see that candlelight is fire, he will mistake glass for pearls:

Just because it is so clear,
It takes us longer to realize it.
If you quickly acknowledge that candlelight is fire
You will find that the rice has long been cooked![63]

If you see the Buddha, kill him.

INTERRELIGIOUS DIALOGUE

> An outsider, a non-Buddhist, questioned the Buddha in these terms: "I do not ask about the spoken, I do not ask about the unspoken."
>
> The Buddha just sat there.
>
> The outsider said in praise, "World Honored One, you are very kind, very compassionate; opening up the clouds of my confusion, you have enabled me to attain penetration." Then he paid respects and left.
>
> Ananda subsequently asked Buddha, "What did the outsider realize, that he uttered this praise and left?"
>
> Buddha said, "Like a good horse, he goes as soon as he sees the mere shadow of the whip."

In Zen language, an outsider is one who clings to anything outside. This includes all notions and opinions about the truth of reality; all that can be conceived (the spoken) and all that can not be conceived (the unspoken). The outsider in this story asks the Buddha if there is any realization that transcends the thinkable and the unthinkable, the relative and the absolute.

While the Buddha just sat there, the reply he gave to the outsider was not the silence of just sitting there because that would have been about the unspoken or the absolute. Rather, the Buddha's "just sitting there" without negating or assenting to anything, led the outsider to penetrate all possible subjective opinions.

The story goes on to compare Ananda, a close disciple of the Buddha, with the outsider. Ananda lived with the Buddha but did not grasp the point of his teaching. The outsider, seeing only the shadow of the whip, awakened directly to what was

real. The question is, therefore, who is the real disciple of the
Buddha? Is it the one who clings to dogmatic opinions about
Buddhism and Zen, or the one who transcends dogma, neither
negating nor assenting, and reaches the heart of the matter?

I chose this koan to ask a vital interreligious question.
Can one with living faith in any non-Buddhist tradition study
Zen with profit, see nature as it is, and even be asked to teach
others? I suggest that this koan affirms that an outsider can see
his or her own nature without having to negate or assent to any
religious opinions whatsoever. Seeing is not the prerogative of
those who grow up in a Buddhist world-view. In fact clinging to
opinions about the Buddhist world view can be disastrous even
for those who sit next to the Buddha himself.

Let us briefly look at interreligious dialogue between Zen
Buddhists and Christians, first from the Christian, and then
from the Zen Buddhist, point of view.

First, when Christians approach Buddhists today we do so
first of all by publicly acknowledging all the sins of our missionary past. We repent of all in our colonial history that resulted in
others seeing us as aggressive, imperialist, and violent. Second,
the conversion Christians hope for is primarily that of Isaiah,
that our hearts of stone might become hearts of flesh ready to
serve God's people in the world. Third, we know that our
attempts at interreligious dialogue since Vatican II show that
neither a purely intellectual nor a purely institutional dialogue
is likely to bear fruit. Rather, we need to place an emphasis on
religious experience, on our actually sitting together; this may
seem less ambitious than our older agenda of intellectual and
institutional exchange, but it is in fact more demanding.
Communal experience combines the theological, social, and
prayerful dimensions of every religion, and it demands hope
and patience from all.

Finally, we must base our interfaith dialogue upon practical action for justice and for the development of marginalized
peoples. The partners in dialogue must look beyond themselves and reach out in compassionate service. Catholics,
therefore, must come to interreligious dialogue to learn, to
share, and to serve.

Buddhism, for its part, has always tried to bridge the cultural and religious gulf it met when it entered a new milieu. For

example, when the Buddhist missionaries left India for China
they faced the enormous barrier of the Chinese language so different from their own. Chinese grammar, vocabulary, literacy
modes, and imagination were often the opposite of the languages of the Indian tradition. The two cultures also differed in
their attitudes toward the individual and in their disposition to
analyze the human personality. In their philosophical concepts
of space and time and in their social and political values, Indian
and Chinese societies developed along divergent paths. It was a
magnificent cultural achievement for the Indians to make
Buddhism a truly Chinese faith. And this achievement was
repeated in Southeast Asia, Tibet, Korea, and Japan. Surely
now that Buddhism has come to America it will continue its
effort to express itself within the values of this country and to
dialogue with its religious traditions. Buddhism, as always,
stands ready to welcome the "outsider" and to invite him to see
for himself.

In his play *St. Joan*, Bernard Shaw has Joan say, "I hear
voices. They come from God." Her friend replies, "They come
from your imagination." Joan answers, "Of course. That is how
the messages of God come to us." Interreligious dialogue is
surely a work of the imagination. It may not be for everyone.
Yet we can imagine that two great contemplative and social traditions can meet as one to enrich each other and to work for the
common good. We can imagine that the riches of centuries of
Buddhist thought and practice can extend the boundaries of the
Christian mind. We can imagine that Buddhist monasticism
can include the insights of Jewish and Christian social teaching
and service. We especially can imagine that Buddhists and
Christians can labor together for justice and sit down together
in peace. And after so much imagining we can spend our lives
making all we have imagined come true.

PART IV

GOLD

ACHIEVEMENT AND UNION

The rearing of the head's horn shows its unworthiness.
A mind set on the quest of Buddhahood is shameful indeed!
Since the far distant empty aeon no one yet has known
That which journeyed south to visit three and fifty sages.

THE BIRDS

Every day Master Zuigan Shigen used to call out to himself, "Oh, master!" And would answer himself, "Yes?" "Are you awake?" he would ask, and would answer, "Yes, I am." "Never be deceived by others, any day, any time." "No, I will not."

A few years ago, a Jesuit friend of mine working in West Africa returned to New York for medical rehabilitation. While he was here he asked me to help him understand Zen; I gave him this koan to work with. My friend found the koan so fascinating that we often used it when we greeted each other. "Are you awake?" Unfortunately this koan of Master Zuigan is more enjoyed than it is truly grasped by the beginning student. On first reading the student can enjoy both the one-man play, and the dramatic dialogue, and conclude that Master Zuigan was giving himself some sound humanistic advice.

The truth of the koan, however, is grasped by answering the question: who is it who is calling out and who is it who is answering? Who is it that appears in different masks? Unless these questions are fully answered, the student's Zen will be repetitious and lifeless.

In order to grasp the truth of Master Zuigan's play, let me present another play, *The Conference of the Birds*, a metaphorical tale of spiritual journey, once narrated by Farid Ud-Din Attar, a twelfth-century Persian poet and mystic. In this play the characters are not calling out and answering, but seeking and finding. Let us consider hear about the birds and their journey to the king.[1]

Attar tells us that all the birds of the world gathered in one place to embark upon a journey to seek a king. They are told by the hoopoe-bird, their sheikh-like guide, that there is indeed a king of royal magnificence who resides in remote and sacred mountains. They are also told that the journey to the king's aerie is long and treacherous.

On their journey the hoopoe-bird tells stories to inspire and intrigue the other birds. As the journey becomes more and more difficult, many birds find excuses to abandon their search. However the others press on "with . . . tattered, trailing wings," evolving in their spiritual awareness and determined to gaze on the beauty of the king.

As the tale unfolds we can distinguish five stages in the birds' evolving awareness of their relationship to the king. Each stage traces a progression in the development of a unitive spirituality which theists can readily identify with. For the non-theistic Buddhist, I would suggest that each of the stages represents a koan to challenge and comfort the pilgrims.

I. GLIMPSING THE KING'S REFLECTED MAJESTY

The first stage in Attar's spiritual theology is the awareness that the greatness of the king demands his being seen only in subdued and reflected majesty. Thus the hoopoe-bird tells of a great king whose charmed majesty is such that none can view his face without languishing always in its absence. Hence the king's counselors devise a way to partially reveal as well as hide the unreflected glory of the king. They place oblique mirrors around the palace so that the king's image will shine before the people with mitigated splendor.

In spite of this solution, the people still long to see what the mirrors hide, and they sense the beauty sometimes found in the least expected places. As a result, they set out to search for the glory lurking beyond the ordinariness of things.

At this stage, a Buddhist might express admiration for this metaphor and add a question of his own: If all the birds search for the One, what does the One search for? Only when I can answer this question will my searching cease. Only then will I know I need not set out to seek a king in remote and sacred mountains.

A Buddhist might paraphrase his question: "If all things return to the One, then even diamonds lose their luster. But if the One returns to all things, what can we say of the pebbles?"

II. Rejoicing in the Weakness of the King

The second stage in the development of Attar's unitive spirituality is the recognition that the king makes himself most vulnerable in love. Here the hoopoe-bird tells the pilgrim birds of a great king riding alone one day and coming upon a small boy fishing from a broken pier. The king dismounts, silently approaches the child and says,"You seem the saddest boy I've ever seen." "Our father is gone," the boy replies. "For seven children I cast my line. Our mother is paralyzed and we are poor. I come to fish here in the dawn's first light. And I cannot leave until the fall of night."

The king sits down beside the boy and asks to be his friend. They sit exchanging stories while the boy pulls in a hundred fish and more. "A splendid haul," the king exclaims as he finally stands to leave. "Wait," says the boy, "take your share. Half the catch is yours." But the king laughs as he rides away.

"Tomorrow's catch is mine. We won't divide today's; you have it all," the king [replies].
"Tomorrow when I fish you are the prey. A trophy I refuse to give away."[2]

The next day, a captain fetches the unknown child. At the king's command he is seated beside the royal throne. Courtiers murmur at the king's reckless love for the worthless waif.

To every taunt the boy has one reply: "My sadness vanishes when the king passes by."[3]

I believe a Buddhist would admire the metaphor of a king caring deeply for that of which he has no need. And I think this metaphor would nudge him to consider a little-known koan that would sharpen his vision even more clearly: One day a retarded monk comes to the Buddha and begs him to lead him to enlightenment. The Buddha has compassion for the poor monk and bids him sit in the north corner of the room where the Buddha tosses a ball to him. Then the Buddha moves the monk to the east corner, then to the south corner and finally to the west

corner, and each time the Buddha tosses the ball to him. At the
end the retarded monk comes to enlightenment.

Similar to the notion that the king should pass one's way
and pause to love is the koan's teasing the Buddhist student to be
clear about who has compassion for whom and about the nature
of the wisdom so gently offered from every point of the compass.

III. Realizing the Possibilities of Boldness in Love

The third stage of Attar's unitive spirituality—the spiritual
journey to the king—is the awareness that one need not wait
passively by the sea for the king to come. In this he agrees with
the Muslims: Allah longs for aggressive lovers and will yield to
an enterprising grasp when he will not bend to bloodless, unim-
passioned service. This image is close to the Jewish thought of
boldness toward heaven, *chutzpah k'lapei shemaya.*

The hoopoe-bird tells the pilgrim birds the tale of an old
crone, coarse and loud but wiser than the waning moon, who
was standing in the crowd that ancient day when Joseph was
sold in Egypt as a slave. The asking price for Joseph was five
whole tubs of musk. The wise old crone perceived the beauty of
the Canaanite boy, pushed through the crowd, and with all her
might shouted out her offer of all she had—a few strands of
twisted threads. The merchant laughed with contempt, but the
woman stoutly answered back:

> I knew you wouldn't sell him for my thread—
> But it's enough that everyone will say
> "She bid for Joseph on that splendid day."[4]

She knew that the heart not bold would never gain access to the
king. We know too that it is the fervor of love that makes the
measure of the soul.

At this stage I picture a Buddhist listening intently and
nodding with appreciation at this praise of boldness in theistic
imagery, and I see him asking the theists a question of his own
which the imagery of the story provoked: How does one step
down from the top of a hundred foot pole?

"Surely with caution," one theist might suggest. "Perhaps
with one great bold leap," another might add. "Only after finding a safe place to land," still another might caution.

I hear the Buddhist exclaiming: "You know caution will never do, and one bold leap is not enough. Nor is there any other safe place to land either here or in some Western land. There is no other one to help us and no other place to go, and yet we must step down from the pole again and again and again . . ."

IV. ABANDONING HOPE AT THE THRESHOLD OF THE KING

In stage four the birds press closer to their goal. Their yearning for the king is heightened by the wondrous tales of the hoopoe-bird, but this stage of their pilgrimage brings them to despair. For the hoopoe-bird tells them that their quest is absurd. They discover that only those who love the king enough deserve to see him, and that those who do love enough will die out of longing for him. Their wings beat furiously on the cage of a paradox they cannot escape; death is a prerequisite to see the king:

> You cannot hope for life till you progress
> Through some small shadow of this Nothingness.[5]

In Sufi thought, the experience of union with God is only achieved through fana or self-annihilation. For the Jews, too, there is no other way to the presence of the king:

> Only as Joseph's brothers are shown and read the bill of sale
> by which they sold their father's son so many years ago—only
> as they sink in hopeless despair, while standing before the one
> they betrayed—can there come the tears of the Egyptian Lord
> who embraces them once again as his own flesh and kin.[6]

Likewise for the Christian, only when his flesh has been nailed to the cross with Christ can he hope to become his disciple. The Buddhist, would agree most emphatically with Attar's metaphor which recalls for him the essential koan of Bodhidharma looking out of his cave at the young man who would be his disciple:

> You would follow the path of the Buddha?
> You, with your easy virtue?[7]

Accordingly, every morning before the sun is up and before any work is done, Buddhist monks renounce all evil karma they

have ever committed. Without this profound renunciation there
is no Buddhism.

Poor birds! They thought all they needed to reach the king
was self-confidence and boldness. Now they are given a paradox, not different from a bill of sale, a crucifixion, and the
uncompromising eyes of Bodhidharma.

V. Discovering Surprise at Union with the King

The fifth and final stage of Attar's unitive theology is one of surprise and mystery. Only thirty birds complete their journey to
the king. (The Persian word for king is *simorgh* which is made
up of two separate words, *si*, for thirty and *morgh*, for bird[s].)
These thirty birds are exhausted, broken things. At the moment
they know themselves at last undone, the door to the grand
chamber of the king is pulled open to the last. A hundred veils
draw back, and there . . .

> Before the birds' incredulous, bewildered
> sight shines the unveiled, the inmost
> Light of Light.[8]

With awe and fear the birds stand before a king they never
would have imagined:

> There in the Simorgh's radiant face they (see)
> Themselves, the Simorgh of the World—with awe
> They (gaze) and (dare) at last to comprehend
> They (are) the Simorgh and the journey's end.[9]

The birds find themselves in undivided unity with the king for
whom they have abandoned all. They know that their distant
king has been closer than home itself. To have thought this at
the start of their journey would have been terrible narcissism.
But now amid the carnage of their broken selves they experience a joyous transformation.

At this final stage Christians remember that St.
Augustine said that at the end there will be one Christ loving
himself; Muslims recall that Abu Yazid al Bistami exclaimed,
"How great is my majesty." Similarly, I hear the Buddhist
exclaim: "To Islam, and all her sheiks and sufis, gassho."

The *Conference of the Birds* brings together the traditions
of Jews, Christians, and Muslims. I believe this story can help
us appreciate the Zen teaching of Zuigan. The calling master
and the answering master are not two but the One Absolute
master who is calling out to himself and answering himself.
Furthermore, Zuigan's master is also our master and this master is present to us here and now. How will we call out to this
master? How will he answer? Or if it helps us, let us forget the
two masters and the thirty birds. They are metaphors used only
to help us unmask our true master and king, green in the wil-
low, red in the flower, and graceful in the bird. An anonymous
Zen master comments beautifully on this koan:

> A water bird comes and goes,
> Leaving no traces at all.
> Yet it knows
> How to go its own way.[10]

NOTES

Preface

1. Stephen J. Duffy, *Encountering the Stranger; Christianity in Dialogue with the World Religions* (New Orleans; Loyola New Orleans Religious Studies, 1994), 12.
2. Robert Kiely, "The Good Heart," *The Tablet* (October 1994): 1245–46.
3. Ibid.

About the Book

1. Hans Kung, *Theology for the Third Millenium* (New York: Doubleday & Company, Inc., 1988), 251.

Part I.
Lead—The Darkness of Knowledge and Theory

1. Philip Yampolsky, *The Zen Master Hakuin* (New York, Columbia University Press, 1971), 99–100.
2. Ibid., 134–35.
3. Ibid., 161.
4. H. Shurmann, *Buddhism: An Outline of Its Teachings and Schools* (Wheaton, Ill.: Theosophical Publishing House, 1974), 140.
5. John Wu, *The Golden Age of Zen*, introduction by Thomas Merton (Taipei: United Publishing Center, 1975), 2.
6. Robert Kennedy, review of William Johnston's *The Still Point*, in *Thought* 182 (Autumn 1971): 452–55.

7. William Johnston, ed., *The Cloud of Unknowing* (St. Meinrad: Abbey Press, 1975), 37.
8. Ibid., 175.
9. Thomas Merton, *Zen and the Birds of Appetite* (New York: New Directions, 1968), 12.
10. Johnston, *The Cloud of Unknowing*, 97.

PART II.
QUICKSILVER—THE POETRY OF INSPIRATION AND DESIRE

1. Han-Shan, *Cold Mountain*, trans. Burton Watson (New York: Columbia University Press, 1970), 68.
2. Ibid., 7–14.
3. Ibid., 66.
4. Ibid.
5. Ibid., 58.
6. Koun Yamada, *Gateless Gate* (Los Angeles, Calif.: Center Publications, 1979), 125.
7. Han-Shan, *Cold Mountain*, 55.
8. Ibid., 69.
9. Ibid., 76.
10. Ibid., 78.
11. Ibid., 80.
12. Ibid., 56.

PART III.
SULPHUR—THE FIRE OF PRACTICE AND TRANSFORMATION

1. Shibayama Zenkei, *Zen Comments on the Mumonkan* (San Francisco: Harper & Row, 1974), 114.
2. T. S. Eliot, "The Wasteland," in *Collected Poems 1909–1962* (New York: Harcourt Brace & World, Inc. 1963), 57.
3. Francis H. Cook, *The Record of Transmitting the Light* (Los Angeles, Calif.: Center Publications, 1991), 68.
4. Shibayama, *Zen Comments on the Mumonkan,*118.
5. Ibid., 86.
6. John Wu, *The Golden Age of Zen* (Taipei: United Publishing Center, 1975), 140–41.
7. C. S. Lewis, *The Inspirational Writings of C. S. Lewis* (New York: Inspirational Press by arrangement with Harcourt Brace, 1987), 288.

8. Wu, *Golden Age of Zen*, 46.

9. Wallace Stevens, "Theory," in *Collected Poems* (New York: Alfred A. Knopf, 1969), 86.

10. A. E. Housman, *Collected Poems* (Toronto, 1956), 173.

11. Emily Dickinson, *The Complete Poems of Emily Dickinson*, ed. Thomas L. Johnson (Boston: Little Brown & Company), 414.

12. Kathleen Raine, "Love Poem," in *Modern British Poetry*, ed. Louis Untermeyer (New York: Harcourt, Brace & World, 1958), 485.

13. Stephen Mitchell, *The Enlightened Mind* (New York: Harper Collins, 1991), 76.

14. Shibayama, *Zen Comments on the Mumonkan*, 214.

15. Dickinson, *The Complete Poems of Emily Dickinson*, 216–17.

16. Ibid., 312.

17. Percy Bysshe Shelley, "Mont Blanc," in *Anthology of Romanticism*, ed. Ernest Bernbaum (New York: The Ronald Press Company, 1948), 864.

18. T. F. O'Meara, "Toward a Subjective Study of Revelation," *Theological Studies* 36 (September, 1975): 401–27.

19. Shibayama, *Zen Comments on the Mumonkan*, 196.

20. Ibid., 209.

21. Raine, "Question and Answer," in *Modern British Poetry*, 484.

22. Louise Bogan, *The Blue Estuaries* (New York: Ecco Press, 1985), 7.

23. Shibayama, *Zen Comments on the Mumonkan*, 215.

24. Thomas Mann, *The Magic Mountain*, trans. H. T. Lowe-Porter (New York: Vintage Books, 1969), 222.

25. Sibayama, 168.

26. Dickinson, *The Complete Poems of Emily Dickinson*, 153.

27. Wu, *Golden Age of Zen*, 46.

28. Quoted by Tom Box in "Penny Lernoux: A Journey of Trust," in *Cloud of Witnesses*, ed. Jim Wallis and Joyce Hollyday (Maryknoll:, N.Y.: Orbis Books, 1991).

29. Dag Hammarskjöld, *Markings* (London, England: Faber and Faber, 1963), 167.

30. Shibayama, 273.

31. John Fowles, *The Ebony Tower* (New York: A Signet Book, 1974), 1–107.

32. Shibayama, *Zen Comments on the Mumonkan*, 82.

33. Daniel Berrigan, *Time Without Number* (New York: The Macmillan Company, 1957), 47.

34. Belden C. Lane, "Fierce Landscapes and the Indifference of God," *The Christian Century* (October 1989): 907–10.

35. Wu, *Golden Age of Zen*, 144–45.
36. Gilbert Murray, *Five Stages of Greek Religion* (New York: Doubleday & Company, 1955), 119.
37. Ibid., 164.
38. John Steinbeck, *The Grapes of Wrath* (New York: Bantam Books, 1966), 82.
39. Margaret Miles, "The Discovery of Asceticism," *Commonweal* CX (January 1983): 40–43.
40. E. E. Cummings, *Collected Poems* (New York: Harcourt, Brace & World, Inc., 1966), 227.
41. Shibayama, *Zen Comments on the Mumonkan*, 122.
42. Ryokan, *Collected Poems*, trans. Burton Watson (New York: Columbia University Press, 1977), 82.
43. Ibid., 66.
44. Ibid., 51.
45. Ibid., 74.
46. Ibid., 61.
47. Shibayama, *Zen Comments on the Mumonkan*, 127.
48. James Joyce, *Dubliners* (New York: The Viking Press, 1967), 36–41.
49. Mary Gordon, *Good Boys and Dead Girls* (New York: Penguin Books, 1991), 78.
50. Gordon, *Temporary Shelter* (New York: Random House, 1987), 168.
51. Cook, *The Record of Transmitting the Light*, 62.
52. Stephen Spender, "Judas Iscariot," in *Modern British Poetry*, 478.
53. Matthew Arnold, "Dover Beach," in *Victorian Age*, eds. John Wilson Bowyer and John Lee Brooks (New York: Appleton-Century-Crofts, 1954), 493.
54. Shibayama, *Zen Comments on the Mumonkan*, 72.
55. Wallace Stevens, "On the Road Home," in *Collected Poems*, 203.
56. Josephine Hart, *Damage* (New York, Ivy Books, 1991), 56.
57. John Fowles, *The French Lieutenant's Woman* (Bergenfield, N.J.: New American Library, 1969), 275.
58. Alfred Lord Tennyson "Maud," in *The Victorian Age*, 113.
59. Philip Yampolsky, *The Platform Sutra of the Sixth Patriarch* (New York: Columbia University Press, 1967), 169.
60. John Wright, "Roger Haight's Spirit Christology," *Theological Studies* 53 (December 1992): 734.
61. Yampolsky, *The Platform Sutra of the Sixth Patriarch*, 180.

62. Teilhard de Chardin, *Le Milieu Divan* (London, England: Fontana Books, 1964), 143.
63. Shibayama, *Zen Comments on the Mumonkan*, 70.

PART IV.
GOLD: ACHIEVEMENT AND UNION

1. Farid Ud-Din Attar, *The Conference of the Birds*, in *Horizons* 14 (Spring, 1987): 111.
2. Ibid., 79–80.
3. Ibid., 79–80.
4. Ibid., 132–133.
5. Ibid., 221.
6. Ibid., 217–18.
7. Shibayama Zenkei, *Zen Comments on the Mumonkan* (San Francisco: Harper & Row, 1974), 287.
8. Farid Ud-Din Attar, *The Conference of the Birds*, 221.
9. Ibid., 219.
10. Shibayama, *Zen Comment on the Mumonkan*, 98.